Fiona & Ulysses

I AM
BRIDE

I AM BRIDE

HOW TO TAKE THE WE OUT OF WEDDING
(and other useful advice)

LAURA WILLCOX

illustrations by JASON O'MALLEY

ABRAMS IMAGE, NEW YORK

Contents

"I think a hero is an ordinary [bride] who finds the strength to persevere and endure in spite of overwhelming obstacles."

—CHRISTOPHER REEVE *(with a little editing by me!)*

Your Big Day

Your wedding day is the most important day of your life.

It is a day to gather with your closest friends and family to celebrate the one and only you and the fact that you found a man to mate with and pay for your expensive taste for as long as you both shall live.

As a high-end wedding planner, I have had the privilege of bearing witness to countless weddings. And yet, I like to think of myself as so much more than a person who plans weddings for a living. I am an artist, a therapist, a creator, and a leader. But at the end of the day, it is the bride who is the true dictator—her wedding is her totalitarian state. And this is exactly as it should be.

One could equate the tradition of a woman's wedding day to that of a Viking funeral. A wedding is the peak of a woman's life, the day after her wedding marking the beginning of a long, onerous trudge to the end. But let's not focus on that right now. Because if you've purchased this book, that means you have a wedding ahead of you, which means your life is currently full of purpose and meaning. Nothing is more important than your wedding, which means if you're a bride-to-be, no one is more important than *you*.

It's also important to note that brides come in all shapes and sizes. Brides don't necessarily have to be female. As long as you are courageous enough to devote your whole life to your wedding, and are able to take full advantage of those around you to get what you want when you want it, then you, my friend, are a bride, male or female. And you need my services.

In this tome you will find a step-by-step guide to help you achieve your dream of the perfect wedding, covering everything from finding the perfect venue to finding the perfect Swarovski crystals for the bodice of your backup wedding dress to finding the perfect way to prevent your future in-laws from being involved in your wedding at all. Allow me the privilege of imparting the wisdom I've curated over my twenty-plus years of planning some of the most extravagant weddings in the tri-state area. Wedding planning is a massive undertaking, so I always recommend that my brides take a permanent leave of absence from their jobs, quit extracurricular activities (especially any volunteer obligations!), and sever ties with any unnecessary friends and family. Your wedding is your life now. Enjoy it!

And should you find yourself in a moment of frustration during the planning process, it's important to remember what this day is all about: *you*. After all, there's no *us* in *wedding*. Yes, there's a *we*, but it's the royal *we*, which means *me* (which means you!). *I Am Bride* shall be your new mantra. And let this book be your guiding light.

FOR THE GROOM

If you've read this far, you've wasted two minutes of your life that you'll never get back. This book is not for you. A groom getting heavily involved in wedding planning is sort of like a monkey trying to ride a tricycle—it's both disturbing and fruitless. And no one cares what kind of cake the groom prefers, so why would you even *mention* you like German chocolate? Once you knelt on the ground and begged for her hand in marriage, your work was done. Now all you have to do is sit back, relax, and enjoy as you discover brand-new sides of the woman you've just asked to be your wife, her full personality finally able to blossom as she settles into her new role as a bride-to-be.

"A journey of a thousand miles must begin with a single step [and an increased credit limit]."

—LAO TZU / *Me*

CHAPTER ONE

Your First Steps

He finally proposed!

If you're still in your twenties, congratulations! You have achieved something that lesser women have failed at for centuries. If you're thirty or older, then read quickly, because you are in a race against death.

The moment you get engaged, something very special happens: You cease being a woman and you become a *bride-to-be*. Your new life begins the moment he slips that ring past the first knuckle—and hopefully he bought the ring that you picked out and emailed a picture of to him once a week! (For more tips on getting a man who isn't ready to propose to finally pop the question, please see my book *Getting What You Want at All Costs.*) Now that you two are happily betrothed, his work is done! But *your* journey has just begun. It's time for you to embark on the most exciting and solitary journey of any woman's life: planning your wedding day.

It's a daunting task for sure. You have one shot to turn your childhood wedding fantasies into reality. It's likely your expectations are unrealistically high—and that's exactly where they should remain! Planning the perfect fairy-tale wedding will require some blood, sweat, and lots of tears. So many tears. So allow me to hold your hand through this process every step of the way.

Let's start at the very beginning. After all, every detail leading up to your wedding is just as crucial as the details of the day itself!

Crafting the Perfect Engagement Announcement for Social Media: Dos and Don'ts

Becoming someone's fiancée is sort of like gaining access to the most exclusive club in town. Think it's hard getting inducted into the Illuminati? Try getting a *man* to commit! Good luck, sister! Reliable sources like sitcoms, rom-coms, and chick lit have taught us for centuries that men hate commitment. So once you do get him down on one knee, it's perfectly natural to want to announce this momentous accomplishment to your extended social network. But there's a right way and a wrong way to do this. The "right" way will make a lot of people jealous; the "wrong" will merely make people happy *for* you, not want to *be* you.

DO use a photo! The ideal photo captures the location of the proposal (as any man worthy of you will have a professional photographer on retainer to capture the engagement), the general vibe of the proposal (surprise, tropical, expensive, romantic), the relief in your eyes that you're not going to die alone,

Got Engaged

The Bride To Be
"I SAID YES! #obviouslyisaidyes #blackmailworks #ultimatumsworktoo

 Like   💬 Comment   ➔ Share

 Susan Single I am so happy for you!!!!!! I am not jealous at all hahaahHAHAHAHA hahahahha ahhhhhhhhhhhhh
Like · Reply · 2 hours ago

 Becky Betch Oh that ring is SO cute! It's like the baby version of mine! Congrats!
Like · Reply · 2 hours ago

 Carrie Coworker There's an office-wide bet that you're pregnant! Mazel!
Like · Reply · 2 hours ago

 Tom Tightwad Shit. ANOTHER wedding I'll have to go to this year. Maybe I can sell my car…
Like · Reply · 2 hours ago

 Eddie the Ex Good luck with her, bro.

and, most important, the ring. Make sure your announcement photo conveys all these things! And if it doesn't, keep taking pictures until you get the right one, no matter how long it takes. You and your fiancé have the rest of your lives to celebrate your engagement together—but you only have *one* chance to get this picture right.

DO utilize all platforms! You want your announcement to reach as many eyes as possible, so post on Facebook, Twitter, Instagram, Snapchat, Tumblr, Ello, Bumble, Pinterest, and Tinder. Don't have enough followers? Those can be bought!

DON'T be afraid to use hashtags! These are a clever marketing secret that can really drive traffic to your engagement announcement. Research has found that the longer the hashtag and the greater the quantity of hashtags used, the better. Some great hashtags to consider:

#blessed
#sohappy
#futuremrsX
#engaged
#helikeditsoheputaringonit
#bridetobe
#hedidntgotoJaredhewentsomewherebetter
#myengagementringcost$36,167justfyi
#imhappierthanyou

DON'T stop posting until you get the number of "likes," "retweets," and "shares" that your engagement announcement deserves! Remember, you're setting the tone for your entire wedding with this post. If your post gets a meager number of "likes" or "shares" (less than five hundred), then ask yourself, "What am I doing wrong?" It might be something simple (your groom isn't photogenic and should be cropped out, your privacy settings are too strict), or it might be a bigger issue (you're unlikable, etc.). Be tenacious.

DO go big! A great set of pictures will certainly suffice, but a viral video is even more memorable! Of course, being proposed to via flash mob takes some foresight on your behalf, because you have to get your future fiancé on board. But assure him that all the hard work will pay off in the end. And let him know you won't accept his proposal without adequate fanfare.

A SPECIAL NOTE ON GETTING INTO THE *NEW YORK TIMES* WEDDINGS SECTION:

Unless you're a quad-racial lesbian couple who met while building yurts for underprivileged farmers in Peru during a yoga/service retreat only to discover you had actually been hallmates back at Yale, don't even bother submitting. Being bougie enough to be featured in the Vows section is a lifelong commitment, and unless you've been working toward this since birth (i.e., were born into a rich family), then it's not gonna happen. If you're feeling discouraged, remember that print is dead! (Except for books, of course.)

Your Engagement Ring

Your ring is so much more than a symbol of his love and devotion. It's an external marketing tool that allows you to *always* be advertising the fact that you're getting married. It's an easy visual cue that puts you above the un-engaged others. Why do you think engagement rings are typically so large and sparkly? Because they have a message to share, and therefore they demand to be noticed. In order to maximize your engagement ring's effectiveness, consider the following tips:

✳ If you're not already a lefty, try to make your left hand your dominant hand. Using your left hand more will give you more opportunities to flash that big sparkler and let everyone around you know, "I am someone's very expensive property!" Whether you're using a fork, brushing your bangs aside, or simply hailing a cab, give those fingers a little wiggle and watch as jealousy seethes just beneath the surface of every woman in your vicinity.

✳ Figure out your ring's best angles and find your ring's best light. Does your square cut do best tilted slightly to the right in natural lighting? Then try to keep a large window to your right as often as possible.

✳ A diamond is a weapon. It's one of the strongest stones on the planet and you can use that to your advantage. Sure, an Instagrammed photo of your ring may last forever, but scarring someone physically by "accidentally" scratching them with your ring is truly forever. They're *never* going to forget that you're engaged! This form of marketing is particularly effective with frenemies.

What Kind of Bride Are You?

Now that you've announced to the world your pending bridedom, it's time to focus on yourself for once. On the following pages you'll find a handy flowchart I've created to help you figure out what kind of bride you are.

WHAT KIND OF BRIDE ARE YOU?

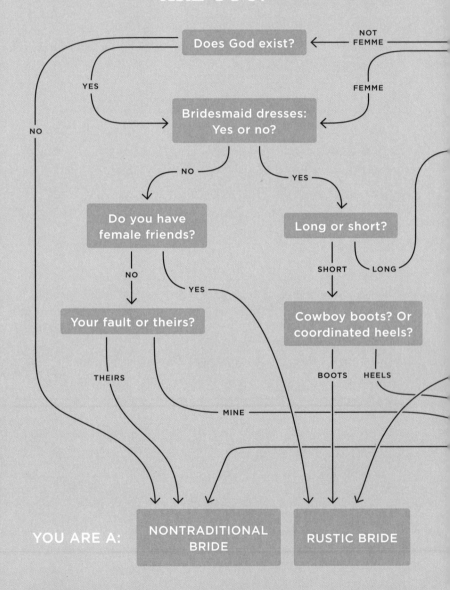

Does God exist?

NOT FEMME

FEMME

YES

NO

Bridesmaid dresses: Yes or no?

NO

YES

Do you have female friends?

Long or short?

NO

YES

SHORT

LONG

Your fault or theirs?

Cowboy boots? Or coordinated heels?

THEIRS

BOOTS

HEELS

MINE

YOU ARE A: NONTRADITIONAL BRIDE   RUSTIC BRIDE

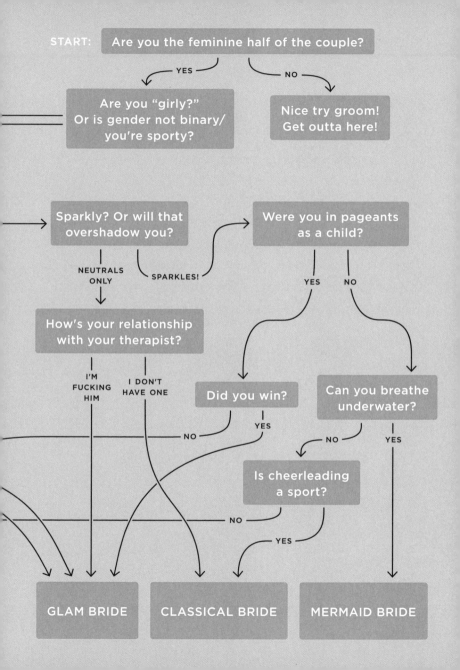

NONTRADITIONAL BRIDE

You're a funky lady who likes to think outside the box and who has an inherent disrespect for tradition. Perhaps you're an artist, yoga instructor, social worker, or member of some other frivolous profession. You'd probably get a kick out of wearing a tea-length, nonwhite wedding dress with shoes of a shockingly bright color—or worse, Converse sneakers. You plan to write your own ceremony, which will most definitely include lighting a soy-based candle to symbolize the fire of your love and at least one poem written by someone with an exotic-sounding name who is in fact just a barista in Portland. At least your wedding will be memorable, because people will have literally no idea what's going on.

RUSTIC BRIDE

Whoa there, cowgirl! To you, glamour is defined by anything that seems a little dirty, used, and obviously cheap. Display bouquets in old coffee tins? Sure! Decorate your wedding with a handmade craft project such as paper bunting? Why not? Get married in a barn that is literally a house for animals? Absolutely! But perhaps you've figured out a secret that other rustic brides before you have long known: You are going to look extra radiant against the shitty backdrop that is your rustic wedding. When you walk down an aisle made of dirt and mulch in this season's Monique Lhuillier, you're going to shine that much brighter.

GLAM BRIDE

To you, nothing is ever good enough. There is no such thing as too much sparkle, too many feathers, too much animal print, too strong a Long Island accent, or too wide a berth that people must make to navigate the girth of your wedding gown. You understand that to be a woman is to be flashy. After all, if angels can be dressed head to toe in feathers, why shouldn't you be? When guests walk into your wedding—or your home, for that matter—you want the decor to be so over-the-top that your guests feel like they've been physically assaulted . . . by beauty! And chandeliers.

CLASSICAL BRIDE

You're an old-school kind of gal living in an ever-modernizing world. You value tradition and have an appreciation for doing things a certain way just because that's how they've always been done. You don't burden yourself with questioning the status quo—after all, worrying causes wrinkles! So go ahead and wear white on your wedding day, toss your bouquet, and let your husband peel a garter belt off your inner thigh with his teeth in front of your relatives. Who cares what any of this symbolizes? You are living proof that ignorance is bridal bliss!

MERMAID BRIDE

You're probably a princess, or at least some sort of sea royalty; not just any mermaid is allowed to marry, procreation being such a difficult and painful process for your kind. You respect the laws of the sea, and no matter who you're marrying—be it a dolphin, wise tortoise, or drowned sailor—you understand that your top priority is to rule with a gentle but decisive hand. But that doesn't mean you can't treat yourself to a Caribbean-style wedding, even if your kingdom is at the bottom of the Mariana Trench. Live a little! After all, you're going to live for two hundred years.

The Guest List

Now this might seem premature, but it's never too early to get started on your guest list. Like a fine glass of Veuve Clicquot, your guest list can easily bubble over if you're not careful. And it will get stale and flat if you put it off too long. Also, your guest list will hopefully be mostly French. *Très chic!*

✳ BRIDESMAIDS: First and foremost, determine who your bridesmaids will be. Choose wisely—who do you want serving you and catering to your every beck and call for the next six to eighteen months? Think of the women or gay men in your life who truly support you, love you, and, most important, are submissive to you. The last thing you want to worry about on your wedding day is some uppity bridesmaid who dares to question your choice of bridesmaid dress—or worse, gets bangs without asking your permission first. Once you've decided that list, it's time for . . .

✳ GROOMSMEN: When compiling the list of acceptable groomsmen for your fiancé, keep in mind that he cannot have more attendants than you, as that will offset the balance of the universe. Limit the list to family and his close friends who won't try to sleep with your bridesmaids. You need your ladies focused on *you*, not their libidos.

✳ EVERYONE ELSE: Only invite the people you actually want to be there. Are there cousins you don't care about whom your parents are insisting you invite? Friends of your groom? Anyone your in-laws know or are related to? Remember, this is *your* day, so you should only be surrounded by people *you* want/love/admire, who won't steal the spotlight from you!

⸕ However, do invite your frenemies. Your wedding day is the first day of your new life with your husband, and it's also the day you're going to look hotter and thinner than everyone else. It's important to have those bitches there so they can stew in their own jealousy. Feeding off of their resentment will only make you stronger.

⸕ In the words of my style icon and life role model Real Housewife Countess LuAnn de Lesseps, "money can't buy you class" . . . but it *can* buy you big wedding presents. Keep income and wealth levels in mind when compiling your guest list.

⸕ When in doubt, make an A-list, a B-list, and a C-list. Place people who almost make the cut on your B-list, and invite them once you've gotten RSVPs from your A-list. The C-list is a great place to put anyone your in-laws or fiancé want to invite. Chances are you won't ever make it to the C-list. It's a win-win—for you at least.

Creating Your Gift Registry

A gift registry is essential for many reasons. We all know the best way for your friends and family to show their love is through material goods. It's also a crucial step in transitioning your home into that of an adult married person. When building your registry, it's important to list items that are practical, such as bedsheets, cooking utensils, and fourteen-karat-gold-plated china, but don't stop there. Make sure to include items you think you *might maybe someday* want, even if you don't want them now. Remember, this is your one and only chance to get literally anything you could ever want purchased for you by your friends and family (until you have a baby, but more on that later).

Here are some oft-overlooked items that *every* bride should register for:

* CARAFE CARAFE. This is a carafe in which to store and display your new wine carafe. Just a slightly bigger carafe that you put your carafe into. Helps keep your wine carafe from getting dusty.

* CHERRY PITTER. You wouldn't want your husband to catch you hand-pitting cherries, now would you?

* STEMWARE. You probably already own wineglasses, but did you know there is a different kind of wineglass for every kind

THE TRADITIONAL GIFT TABLE

diamond wine opener

daybed sheets

avocado baskets

cherry pitter

THANK

carafe carafe

monogrammed
toilet paper

lonely
robot butler

Y O U

of wine? Serving pinot gris in a glass designed for pinot noir is a great way to ruin a perfectly good glass of pinot gris.

* AVOCADO BASKETS. These are baskets specially designed to hold avocados. But note that they will not hold any other items, only avocados.

* DIAMOND WINE OPENER. This is for decoration only, as it would shatter any wine bottle into a billion pieces (except for diamond wine bottles, of course).

* DAYBED SHEETS. When registering, brides often forget linens for their daybeds. Also, linens and decorative pillows for fainting couches and foyer stools, as well as monogrammed bidet covers.

* MONOGRAMMED TOILET PAPER. (To match your bidet cover.)

* ROBOT BUTLERS. You'll need at least two so they don't get lonely when you aren't home.

A SPECIAL NOTE ON DONATIONS IN LIEU OF GIFTS:
It's unfortunate, but some well-meaning albeit misguided guests may make a donation in your name in lieu of a wedding gift. If this happens, remain calm. Sit the offenders down, and

gently explain to them why what they did is so stupid. A donation is useless to you, and they basically just threw away their money. Remind them they have a year to get you a new wedding gift, as etiquette dictates.

Creating a Wedding Budget

It's no secret: Weddings are expensive! Between paying for venues, vendors, violins, and vajazzling, the costs add up fast. Here's a simple guide to making a wedding budget that will help simplify the process:

1. Turn on your laptop.
2. Open up Microsoft Excel.
3. Go to File, then Save, and save your spreadsheet as "My Wedding Budget."
4. Drag the "My Wedding Budget" file into the trash.
5. Close your laptop.

The truth is, there cannot be a budget. This is your *wedding day*. You cannot work within the confines of a budget. Did Michelangelo worry about a budget when painting the Sistine Chapel? Did Melania Trump worry about a budget when covering her penthouse entirely in Italian marble and gold? Do you think Anne Fletcher, director of the award-winning film *27 Dresses*, worried about money when she was making her masterpiece? *No*. Your wedding is your magnum opus. It is your life's Great Work. You need to be able to follow your heart, no matter the price tag.

There is a plethora of ways to get money to appear out of thin air. You can take out a loan, take out a second mortgage, pawn stuff, steal a bike, or refinance almost anything. Like I always say, where there's a will, there's a way. And if you can inherit some money from a wealthy relative's will, all the better.

When Money Truly Is Scarce

While only about 1 percent of my clients have ever been non–1 percenters, I recognize that not everyone has a wealthy fiancé or a backup trust fund they can turn to when it comes time to pay for their wedding. Traditionally it is the bride's father's responsibility to pay for the whole wedding. This stems from the days when unmarried daughters couldn't work outside the home and were therefore a financial burden on their families. So a father would, in essence, pay a man to marry her with an extravagant wedding. Nowadays this still holds true, with the slight caveat that women *can* work outside the home, some just choose not to. Or they get unpaid internships in PR. Unfortunately not everyone is blessed with a wealthy father. So what are they to do? Scale back their wedding? Blasphemy. This is not an option.

The truth is, the money is out there for the taking; you just have to find a way to access it. And the key is through crowd sourcing. Crowd sourcing has become an immensely popular way to beg people to pay for stuff that you don't want to pay for yourself. Indie films, inventions, medical bills, you name it— if you can fill out the prompts on a Kickstarter site, then other people's money is as good as yours.

Or is it?

You see, the key to a good crowd-sourcing campaign is your video. This is where you will introduce the public, or "suckers," to your cause, convincing them to open up their hearts and their wallets. All good crowd-sourcing videos must contain:

1. HIGH PRODUCTION VALUE. This means hiring a professional crew to write, light, shoot, and direct your video. This will cost a ton of money but just fold those costs into the amount you're asking for.

2. A GOOD STORY. If someone's going to watch a video and donate to a cause, it's not going to be just because you entertained them for five minutes. To use an industry term, you need a "hook." Is it that your husband is being shipped overseas and you want to have a beautiful wedding in Puerto Vallarta before he goes? Is it that his deceased grandmother

always wanted him to get married in a castle in France so you're doing this in honor of her? Or maybe you've wanted 98° to play at your wedding since you were a little girl but that will require springing a couple of them from rehab and that won't be cheap. You can make up whatever sob story you want! It just has to be heart-wrenching enough to rise above all the other riffraff on the Internet.

3. GET A CELEBRITY INVOLVED. This is crucial. The number-one reason people donate to crowd-sourcing campaigns is because they want to feel like they're a part of something cool. If you can get a celebrity to donate and share your video it will guarantee that you'll meet your goal, as people will mindlessly do anything a celebrity asks them to do. It makes them feel a bit closer to their favorite star and briefly takes them out of their overwhelmingly uninteresting lives.

Follow these steps and you'll be well on your way to coercing strangers into funding your dream wedding, just like a true princess!

FOR THE GROOM

Despite the fact that I explicitly told you to stop reading, I am aware that there are some grooms out there who insist on involving themselves in the wedding planning process. And thanks to you, my editor has forced me to write a section in each chapter catered to these men in the spirit of "inclusivity" and "broader appeal."

So for you, the groom who wants to feel involved, here's a fun activity to keep your curious hands and mind busy! See if you can connect the dots to discover the hidden image!

A It's the thing that you bought her that got this whole thing started!

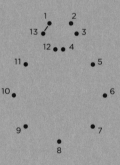

B This is a healthy way to cope with the stress of paying for a wedding!

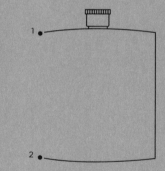

C Don't forget to mark this as "married / filing jointly" from now on!

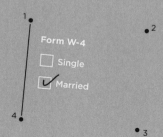

"Is that a *yes* to this dress?"

—ANONYMOUS TV SHOW

CHAPTER TWO

The Look and Feel of Your Wedding

It's time to bring your wedding to life.

That means pushing it down your proverbial birth canal. This can be overwhelming to some. As they say, the devil is in the details. But what's so bad about the devil? I've been called a "white devil" by literally millions of nail technicians, and I think I'm great!

It is true that you have a mountain of small choices ahead of you that will affect the look and feel of your wedding. They are as critical as the decisions a doctor makes when he is delivering a baby. Think of this wedding as *your* baby: Will you let it be born in some inflatable tub in the middle of a living room with a doula chanting nonsense nearby? Or will you welcome it into the world at a state-of-the-art hospital with all the bells and whistles and IVs and thingy-doodads that do God knows what but cost a lot and look important? I think you know the answer.

In this chapter I will walk you through the necessary steps to make sure your wedding has a look and feel that is completely unique and personal to you, while still being homogeneous and indistinguishable from all the weddings you've been pinning on Pinterest.

The Venue

Think of your wedding venue as the hearth and home of your big day. The location of your wedding sets the tone for the entire occasion. There is a wide range of options out there, so you must weigh them carefully when choosing your venue:

TRADITIONAL CHURCH OR TEMPLE WEDDINGS

Even in today's godless, heathen society, religious ceremonies are still quite common. However, church or temple ceremonies mean guests will need to be transported from the ceremony to the reception, and often there is an awkward chunk of time in between the two so you and your bridal party and family can take beautifully staged photographs in an idyllic setting. Some brides stress over this large time period, but I always ask them, "What would Jesus do?" He would walk! They didn't have cars back then. Having guests walk from the church to the reception is a great way to help them pass the time, look slim in the background of your *big day* photos, and work up an appetite!

THE RUSTIC CHIC BARN WEDDING

Barn weddings are more and more popular these days, but unfortunately, due to the slow demise of the farming industry, there are fewer and fewer actual barns available to get married in. This is a great opportunity to DIY your own barn by hiring Amish workers. They're fast, efficient, and cheap because they can't use computers to check out their competitors' prices. These savings are crucial because a barn wedding requires you to rent everything: every napkin, plate, fork, salad fork, caviar fork, food-accidently-dropped-on-the-floor fork, clanking-your-glass-to-kiss fork, grapefruit fork, New York fork, dessert fork, dinner fork, Björk fork, cake fork, plate fork, spork—and even chairs.

TO TENT OR NOT TO TENT?

Unless you're a circus performer or hosting a summer music festival, tents are unacceptable. Sure, you can hang a hundred chandeliers inside a tent—my minimum number of chandeliers for any wedding—but why get married in a venue that is only suitable for dancing to music from the electro house genre while rolling on Molly or for watching adults wearing clown makeup humiliate themselves in exchange for paychecks while rolling on Molly? If you want to have your wedding out-side, have it *outside*! If your guests get rained on, that's their problem. You will have a designated umbrella holder, aka your maid of honor. Remember, this is *your* big day! You can't be expected to worry about whether your guests will get wet.

QUIRKY VENUES

Even offbeat women are getting married these days, which means wedding venues are getting quirkier and more whimsi-cal. Use your imagination! People can get married in museums,

on boats, in sports stadiums, in artisanal mayonnaise shops, on mountaintops, in strangers' backyards, or even on Mexican beaches. Basically, anywhere you want to have a wedding, you can! There is a legal loophole that dictates, much like pirate code, that if a bride wants to have a wedding somewhere—even on private property—then the owners must comply! If they don't, they are subject to constant harassment from the bride until they acquiesce.

Wedding Colors

I am always shocked when I meet brides who aren't aware that they are supposed to choose wedding colors. If your wedding has no color scheme, how can you expect it to be cohesive? Have you ever been to a wedding where the bride's sash doesn't match her table runners? It's a disaster. So choosing the wedding colors should be one of the first decisions you make. Everything else will fall into place from there.

Some suggestions for beautiful colors that look wonderful together:

* Gold and silver
* Blush, medium champagne, and white
* Mint green, raspberry red, and ethnic brown
* Neon pink, lime green, and peacock blue
* Moody yellow, bleak red, canapé pink, and purple stink

* Kale, khaki, and kolorado krimson
* Mustard, chambray, denim, and jeans
* Cucumber seed green-blue, baby blue, big boy blue, and adult green (looks blue)
* Light white, dark white, and deep, unsettling black
* Silver-gray, gray-gold, and goldie hawn

Your Wedding Dress

Gone are the days when all women wore the same boring white dress down the aisle—one with a high neck and long sleeves. Thanks to feminism, there are many ways to individualize your wedding dress so that it is unique to you! For starters, there are more than two hundred different kinds of white to choose from, so you can find the best shade of white for you!

Here are some other popular dress styles to try:

1. BALL GOWN WITH A SWEETHEART NECKLINE: This dramatic, stunning, attention-grabbing gown says, "I'm a sweet little princess . . . who is probably from Long Island!"

2. BALL GOWN WITH A STRAIGHT NECKLINE: Ideal for more conservative brides, this gown says, "I'm refined and quiet and a little bit boring, but still a princess."

1 ball gown
with a
sweetheart
neckline

4 ball gown
with a
boat neck

2 ball gown
with a
straight
neckline

5 ball gown
with a
portrait
neck

3 ball gown
with a
v-neck

6 ball gown
with a
mermaid
cut

3. BALL GOWN WITH A V-NECK: This look is great for women with larger busts, and says, "I'm a princess with a larger bust."

4. BALL GOWN WITH A BOAT NECK: A classic preppy look, perfect for boat, yacht, horse, or Caucasian-themed weddings. This dress says, "I'm a rich princess."

5. BALL GOWN WITH A PORTRAIT NECK: This flattering gown is ideal for women of many body types, especially those that are ashamed of their shoulders. This dress says, "I'm a princess with bad little shoulders."

6. BALL GOWN WITH MERMAID CUT: This risqué or "slutty" silhouette is ideal for the more daring bride, or for a bride who is half woman, half sea creature. This dress says, "I am a princess of the sea, and my dad is King Triton—and I am not afraid to show off my curves!"

Getting Your Body Dress-Worthy with Diet and Exercise

When considering the look of your wedding, you mustn't neglect how YOU look. After all, what do all princesses have in common? They're skinny, and your wedding is telling us a fairy tale about a prince finding his princess—we need to believe you're worth battling an evil witch/dragon/baron over! And that means sticking to a strict diet and exercise plan. Sure, it'll rob your life of any joy, but as they say, nothing tastes as good as being validated for how you look feels!

Here are five tips for making a diet and exercise plan to achieve your most bridetastic bod!

IDENTIFY TROUBLE SPOTS!

Figure out which parts of your physical being you like the least. Is it your flabby arms? Your rotund derriere? Your fat clavicle? If you don't like these parts of yourself, think how we must feel having to look at them all the time! Once you identify everything that's wrong with you, it's time to get to work!

SET A SCHEDULE AND STICK TO IT!

Sure, you're busier than ever now that you're juggling changing your body with planning a wedding. But working out must be a top priority! This is why putting the rest of your life on hold is so important—you can't miss a personal trainer session just because a life event like a funeral pops up. That person is dead, and that shouldn't stop you from living your life! When you pull on that size-zero dress on your wedding day, what is going to make you happier? The memory of being present at your niece's birth or the deep fulfillment and happiness that can only come from being thin? The choice is obvious.

When it comes to working out, setting realistic goals is your key to success. A short three-hour daily workout should be manageable for anyone. Take a look at your schedule and think about what can go to make room for this. Perhaps you have to take a leave from book club, maybe now is the time to take that sabbatical, or perhaps it just means starting your life as a stay-at-home mom now, years before you have a child. Do whatever it takes to carve out time!

STOP EATING AND START BURNING CALORIES!

It's simple, really—eating *adds* calories and that's the opposite of what you want! Your body has grown dependent on burning carbs and fats and proteins for energy, and it's time to break this cycle! The human mind is a powerful muscle—work it to your advantage. Let self-loathing and a fear of failure be your break-fast as you push through that 6 A.M. HIIT session!

SIGN A FITNESS PRENUP

Your future husband needs to understand that you're about to get really, really hot. And that on your wedding day you're going to reach your full hotness potential. But it's import-ant for him to understand that this is not to be expected of you throughout the rest of your marriage. Commit your fitness goals in writing and have him sign it so that he understands that while this is what your free time will be devoted to for the time being, once the wedding is over you're free to let yourself go.

FIGURE OUT YOUR TRIGGERS!

Each person is unique. But what we all have in common as humans is that a self-hatred spiral is the key to our motivation. That's what is going to keep you on that elliptical for an extra hour, and that's what will propel you out of bed at four in the morning to hit the gym, unable to sleep after a night of unsettling dreams. You know, like the recurring one where you're chasing your mother down a long, ornate hallway, calling her name, wishing she'd just turn around and pick you up, hold you, comfort you because you're her *child* dammit and that's what mothers are supposed to do. But she doesn't turn around. She ignores you. Maybe she can't hear you? You scream a little louder. You try to run as fast as you can but your body won't obey and you move as slow as molasses. Pretty soon your mother is so far down the hallway that she's just a tiny pinprick, receding into the darkness. You wake with a start, covered in sweat, ready to hit the pavement for a ten-mile run to drown out the critical voices in your head . . . all of which will bring you that much closer to a slammin' wedding bod!

Bridesmaids and Their Dresses

Choosing bridesmaids' dresses is almost as hard as choosing bridesmaids themselves, and twice as important. After all, if your bridesmaids are wearing mismatched dresses or— God forbid—dresses with different hemline lengths, then the entire ceremony will be completely ruined. Here are some tips to make this decision less fatiguing for you!

CONSIDER YOUR OWN DRESS

Remember, you are the star of the show! So your bridesmaids' dresses should be plainer, simpler, and overall less flattering than yours. They should be a little too big, with a cut not quite right for anyone's body shape, and in a material that looks definitively cheaper than that of your dress without actually being cheap. Of course, keep in mind that cost shouldn't factor into this. If one of your bridesmaids doesn't want to spend a lot of money on her dress, she shouldn't have been born female.

BE MINDFUL OF SKIN TONE

Since the bridesmaids' dresses should help your bridesmaids blend into the background of your ceremony, it's important to find that perfect dress color that will make the bridesmaids look washed out, but not *too* washed out; we don't want guests thinking you have sickly friends. It's a delicate balance. But at no point should you sacrifice your vision for the day! So if you want to go with, say, a beige-mauve for your elegant fall wedding, then you must stick to that decision. And that may mean letting go of any bridesmaids who look a little too amazing in that color.

CONSIDER THEIR BODY TYPES

Give them a good long thought. Close your eyes and picture them. Are there any bodies that aren't bringing you joy when you imagine your maids walking down the aisle, essentially setting the tone for your ceremony before you even appear? If so, then you need to either ax them or ask them—gently!—to change their bodies. One subtle way is to send them a bridesmaid dress in a size 2 with a cute note that says, *Fit into me by May 9!* Or, if some of your maids are shorter than the others, send them a brochure for tibia implants. Remember: Breast implants can be removed, but a wedding photo of a flat-chested bridesmaid is forever.

BE SPECIFIC

This is especially important for any bridesmaids who live far away and are too selfish to sublet a place to be near you in the months leading up to the wedding. For example, if you are gracious and brave enough to let the women choose their own salmon-colored dresses, it's best to send a swatch. You wouldn't want your maid to show up the day of the wedding in a rosé, peach, or rose-colored dress—or worse, a pink one! That would be an actual waking nightmare of monstrous proportions.

DON'T BE AFRAID TO CHANGE YOUR MIND!

This is your day, so you are allowed to change your mind as often as you want! In fact, changing your mind a lot is a great way to assert dominance over the pack and establish yourself as the alpha. Maybe you once thought you wanted your bridesmaids' look to be Audrey Hepburn meets southern cotillion but now you're more feeling Tinkerbell meets Kate Middleton's college years? Then tell your bridesmaids to buy new dresses! And if they complain or whine, cut them right out of the wedding. Such behavior cannot be tolerated.

Flowers

A question I get more and more from brides these days is, "Do I need flowers?" I always tell them the same thing: Would you ever get a steak au poivre without the poivre? Purchase a Louis Vuitton luggage set without the matching hatbox? Decorate your living room without an original painting by George W. Bush? The answer is no. So you shouldn't have a wedding without flowers unless you want your wedding to feel dead and pointless.

The simple truth is wedding florists are expensive—but they are *critical* to your wedding's success. Any jackass with a vase and a pair of shears can throw together a bouquet, but a wedding florist is a true flower artiste and is therefore worth the expense. Finding the right florist is a delicate tête-à-tête, and your initial conversations should feel like a mating ritual—but the question is, who is wooing whom? You may be surprised.

To help demonstrate the best way to approach and land a high-end wedding florist, thus initiating one of the most important relationships of your life, below is an actual email conversation between one of my favorite florists and one of my brides. I have not changed their names, as anonymity is for cowards.

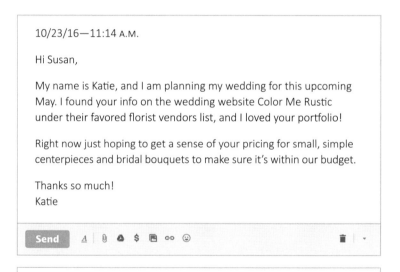

10/23/16—11:14 A.M.

Hi Susan,

My name is Katie, and I am planning my wedding for this upcoming May. I found your info on the wedding website Color Me Rustic under their favored florist vendors list, and I loved your portfolio!

Right now just hoping to get a sense of your pricing for small, simple centerpieces and bridal bouquets to make sure it's within our budget.

Thanks so much!
Katie

Send

10/23/16—4:30 P.M.

Hi Katie,

Thanks so much for reaching out to us at Blossoming Bride! May is such a wonderful time of year for flowers—you chose well! As far as pricing, it would be impossible to quote any prices without first knowing a few more things about you:

How many centerpieces? How many bridesmaid bouquets/boutonnieres? Color scheme? Favorite flowers? Are you Jewish? When's the last time you cried? What's 13 + 46? Where do dogs go when they die? How many fingers am I holding up? And lastly, do you have a wedding Pinterest page? If you don't I'm afraid we can't work together, because we'll simply never see eye to eye.

Thanks! I look forward to hearing from you soon.

Best,
Susan

10/24/16—10:48 A.M.

Hi Susan,

Thanks for getting back to me. Even if you have a broad range of prices, it would be really helpful to know, just to get an idea. But answers to your questions below!

15, 5/7, mint green/ice white, carnations, half, about 5 minutes ago, 59, a cat-themed amusement park in the sky where all the rides are made of bacon, 4 fingers and a thumb, and yes, I have a Pinterest page, but I haven't pinned anything—does that count?

Thx again for taking the time!
Katie

10/24/16—12:04 P.M.

Hi Katie,

Thanks for answering those questions—it's incredibly helpful.

So as for pricing, we start at a minimum of $15K for all events, which would cover the bare minimum required to make your wedding spectacular. (Please note: We can only guarantee spectacular flowers. We have no control over the quality of the food, groom, or weather.)

From your answers I can tell you are someone who would love a rustic and natural arrangement of peonies, anemones, succulents, and ranunculus at each table. Something simple and elegant—just like you!

I'd love to get together to talk about options. Looking forward to it!

Susan

10/24/16—12:15 P.M.

Hi Susan,

Wow, unfortunately $15K is way outside of our budget—we were hoping to spend closer to $2K. Can I ask what all the $15K covers? Forgive me, it just seems like an exorbitant amount of money.

But you're actually right. Once I googled all those names—those are flowers I need and now cannot imagine my wedding day without.

Sorry for all the questions!
Katie

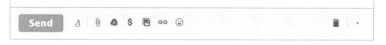

10/24/16—3:13 P.M.

Hi Katie,

I understand. $15K may seem high, but it's pretty standard for most wedding florists. That price includes the cost of all flower arrangements, the air between the flowers, all the dirt (flowers require a *lot* of dirt—and we only use the best dirt full of great worms), as well as the setup and delivery.

We at Blossoming Bride ensure that we'll have the highest-quality flowers imaginable by singing to them on a daily basis, which is way more effective than simply talking to them. Remember Charlotte Church? She was a child opera singer who was big in the '90s? Well, she's exclusively a flower-singer now. We find that the flowers really prefer her voice and she helps them bloom more fully. So that price also covers her services, meals, transportation, and of course flowers for her studio. We are the *only* florist to provide this kind of service in the whole world!

We have found that our brides really appreciate the extra level of detail we put into our work, and that is what makes us stand out from all the other bad, stinky, stupid wedding florists out there.

Let me know if you have any further questions—and I *will* be meeting you soon. It is foretold.

Warmly,
Susan

10/25/16—9:50 A.M.

Hi Susan,

Thanks for clarifying. I love the fact that they're happy, cultured flowers with an appreciation for music, which is so important to me now that I know that such a thing even exists.

I'd love to figure out a way to work with you. Is there anything else you can throw in for us? That might make the sum easier to stomach.

Sorry to be a pain!
Katie

10/25/16—11:28 A.M.

Hi Katie,

You are being a total pain in the ass, so I appreciate your apology.

Here's what I can do for you: I'll waive the fee for our Gift Protection Policy, which is an insurance policy we offer that protects you from having your wedding gifts stolen by me or my associates on the night of your wedding if we are stricken by a case of mischievousness. We recommend this policy to all our clients because we've found that we rob up to 85% of the weddings that don't purchase this protection.

And for what it's worth, all of our brides agree that the look of jealousy on their guests' faces when they see our flowers is worth so much more than $15K. But you already know that. Do the right thing.

Susan

10/26/16—9:08 A.M.

Susan,

I discussed it with my fiancé, and we agree we can just sell his guitar collection and move to a crappier neighborhood. We've realized the flowers are by far the most important aspect of our wedding day.

Looking forward to working with you! Excited!

Your humble servant,
Katie

Send   A | 🖊 ⬥ $ 🖼 ∞ ☺   🗑 | ▾

10/26/16—6:06 P.M.

Hi Katie,

I knew you'd come around. They always do.

I will start putting together a vision board for your wedding today! And I'll need that 50 percent deposit ASAP to hold the date. I only accept payment in the form of Alaska Airlines miles.

MUUUAAHAHAHAHA,
Susan

Send   A | 🖊 ⬥ $ 🖼 ∞ ☺   🗑 | ▾

As you can see, it took some time, but Katie did eventually give herself over to the wise and all knowing florist, and her wedding was a spectacular success because of it! She and her husband are living happily ever after in their twice-refinanced home, with beautiful memories of their wedding flowers that will last a lifetime! The memories, not the flowers. Those, of course, are long dead.

God Is in the Details

By now you are probably suffering from decision fatigue. But there are many smaller details that you mustn't let slide just out of laziness. These details may seem small—to an idiot. Because in reality they will define your wedding—and, if done improperly, ruin it. So they are well worth the tears, stress, time, and money.

WELCOME BAGS

These are crucial for all of your guests who are coming in from out of town to attend your wedding. A welcome bag can be placed in guests' rooms and should contain just a few of the essentials they'll need in order to feel welcome at your wedding: waters with personalized labels with your and your groom's name on them, wine bottles with personalized labels, Advil pills in the shape of your initials (especially if you're getting married in

Thank you all so much for traveling to the world's most remote island of Tristan da Cunha for our wedding! We know it was worth it! We have a fun weekend of MANDATORY activities for you!

Friday:
6:00–7:00 A.M.: Morning mural painting. We'll all be painting our engagement photo onto the side of the local church. But shhh! We didn't get permission from the town so this must be completed before sunrise! There will be mimosas :)

7:30–9:30 A.M.: Group water polo tournament. Let's get to know each other and burn some calories while we're at it! Floaties available for children/non-swimmers.

9:30–11:30 A.M.: Speeches Round 1. A mic and speaker will be available for anyone so moved to speak. Don't worry, there will be twelve more chances to give a speech before the wedding!

11:30 A.M.–12:30 P.M.: Wardrobe approval. The bride will be approving all wedding guest attire so bring options!

continued →

Vegas), an itinerary of the wedding weekend, umbrellas with your initials and wedding date on them, iPhone cases with your initials on them, and a photo of the bride and groom in case guests forget whose wedding they're attending. A personalized tote is the ideal vehicle for your welcome bag, as everyone loves a tote bag with someone else's name and wedding date printed on it!

AMENITIES BASKETS

These are baskets of crucial items to be placed in the bathrooms at the reception venue, and they will make sure your guests are prepared for any possible mishap or situation. So you *must* include all of the following items: combs, bobby pins, Band-Aids, tampons, pads, industrial-size pads, adult diapers, hair spray, hair remover (Nair), socks, shoes, umbrellas, plastic couch covers, cocktail dresses in sizes 0 to 12, a puppy for morale, a cat for "cat people," a signed album from One Direction (before Zayn left), life insurance waivers, one log of uncut pepperoni, and grape-flavored Bubblicious bubble gum.

PARTY FAVORS

Favors are often considered "optional"—but they are far from it. Favors are a way to not only thank your guests for coming but also show off how thoughtful you are by spending money on something 80 percent of the party won't want. Here are some popular favors and what they say about *you.*

✳ HOMEMADE JAM: It doesn't matter that you don't own a farm, that you don't ever cook, and that no one even likes jam. Giving away a monogrammed jar of homemade jam is the quickest way to ensure that your guests will know just how thoughtful and twee you are.

✳ HANDMADE CANDLES IN VINTAGE TEACUPS: They're practical, they're beautiful, they're something everyone wants, and they're easy to make. Simply buy two hundred candles, melt them down, save the wicks, pour the hot wax into two hundred vintage teacups, place wicks in them, let each harden one at a time as you hold the wick in place, transport to your venue without breaking, and voilà! You have two hundred vintage teacup candles that suit all tastes. It's that easy!

✳ PERSONALIZED BOTTLES OF HIGH-END LIQUOR: These are really the ideal wedding favor, as they practically scream at your guests, "I am a fun person!" They're a great way to remind old friends how entertaining you used to be while simultaneously impressing your picky in-laws with the astronomical price point of such a party favor.

✳ FLIP-FLOPS / SANDALS: A basketful of flip-flops or sandals is a thoughtful favor for all the ladies attending your wedding, as it gives them something to bring home and gift to their nannies, cleaning ladies, and housekeepers.

FOR THE GROOM

Fuckin' Yankees, am I right? When are they going to develop their farm system again? Two words: Gene Michael. Never forget it was Gene who kept the Core Four (Jeter, Mo, Pettitt, Posada) together, NOT Steinbrenner! We've got to develop that farm system! Let's take a shot in honor of the 1998 Yankees because OH MY GOD ARE YOU REALLY STILL READING THIS?! This is exhausting.

Here, just look at this picture of a ball for a while:

"Smile knowing you are part of something
infinitely bigger than yourself."

—A REMINDER TO YOUR GUESTS BY RACHEL WOLCHIN

CHAPTER THREE

Share Your Joy

By now your wedding is like a tsunami:

inevitable and devastating (in its beauty). The date has been set, the deposits are paid, and the brides-maids' diet plans have been carefully mapped out for them. Now it's time to share the joy of your wedding with the few, the proud, the chosen who get to attend.

This is my very favorite step. Imagine your wedding guests' delight when they remove your save-the-date magnet from its recycled kraft paper envelope, butterflies in their stomachs, as the words whisper across their lips: "*I get to attend* her *wedding.*"

Did you just get chills, too?

In this chapter I am going to run you through all the steps necessary to share the joy of your wedding with others, whether they are invited guests or just former coworkers who still follow you on Facebook. Because a wedding that isn't well documented is just a very expensive fart in the wind.

looking coyly over her fiancé's shoulder

looking coyly at the camera while being kissed on the forehead

looking coyly at her own reflection in a mirror, which is looking coyly back at her

Save-the-Dates and Invitations

Save-the-dates (STDs) and invitations (I's) may seem like unnecessary redundancies, and maybe they are . . . if you're throwing a birthday party for some shitty toddler. This is your wedding, and a save-the-date is a courteous way to allow your guests ample time to emotionally, physically, and financially prepare for your wedding day. STDs are traditionally mailed out anywhere from six months to a year ahead of time and are an effective way to mark your territory, taking a proverbial piss on that day in the lives of your guests.

WHEN DESIGNING YOUR SAVE-THE-DATES

✳ Your STD should of course feature an engagement photo taken by a professional photographer. Here are some poses that my research has shown to be most flattering for everyone:
  ✳ the bride-to-be looking coyly over her fiancé's shoulder
  ✳ looking coyly over her own shoulder
  ✳ looking coyly at the camera while being kissed on the forehead
  ✳ looking coyly at the camera underneath a cloud of freshly tossed fall leaves
  ✳ looking coyly at her own reflection in a mirror, which is looking coyly back at her

✳ Your STDs should be simple and small enough to be easily spread around to all of your guests, most often transmitted via the USPS. A clever or humorous photo can help your STD go viral—and we all know the most memorable and lasting STDs are the viral ones!

✳ It should be a magnet. Sure, they're more expensive than, say, a postcard, but think of it this way: Your save-the-date can remain front and center on your guests' refrigerators for months. Studies show that eating brings people joy (I wouldn't know), and if your guests see your save-the-date every time they go to open the refrigerator door, they will develop a Pavlovian response to your wedding, associating it with the joy of eating. This is why drooling is common at weddings, especially among uncles.

WHEN DESIGNING YOUR INVITATIONS

✳ Invitations should feel more formal than your STDs, and there is very specific wording that you *must* use. Why? Because that's just how it is. Don't like it? Literally no one cares about your opinion. So the wording should be as follows:

Dr. & Mrs. [*bride's parents full name*]
request the distinct, undeniable, and magnificent
honor and pleasure of your presence at
the marriage of their daughter,

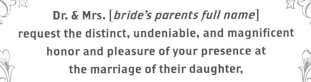

[bride's first name,
middle name(s),
and Catholic name],

[groom's title, first name,
middle name, and last name],

son of Mr. & Mrs. [*groom's parents, name of
country club they belong to*], as they gather
together in God's presence to decree this union
before all that come before them to behold
its great greatness and forever and ever in
holitude amen. Held at Our Lady of Perpetual Sin
Catholic Church on the twenty-ninth of February
in the two thousandth year of our lord plus
seventeen years at exactly six-thirty post meridien.
Dinner and dancing to follow.

✳ Remember that there cannot be a *single numerical digit* anywhere on the invitation. All numbers must be *spelled out*. This is *very important*! If people see numbers they will be confused and upset! This includes the dates, times, addresses, and overall price tag of your wedding (should you choose to include that).

✳ Your invitation should include as many extra cards with information as possible. Ideally, a wedding invitation contains roughly three to twelve cards stuffed into one giant envelope. Such cards include a reception card stating redundantly that you are holding a reception, hotel information, driving directions for guests who don't yet know about the Internet, RSVP cards, brunch information cards, registry information cards, rehearsal dinner information cards, a preemptive thank-you card, an AARP card for movie ticket discounts, a birthday card, a sympathy card, a red card from an intramural soccer game, and a card that states simply, "I'm getting married," just as a reminder. If your envelope weighs less than three pounds at the time of mailing, you've done something dreadfully wrong.

✳ Go big! Don't let your wedding invitation get lost in the fray! Include some sort of cute token that relates to the theme of your wedding. If it's a beach wedding, include a bag of wet sand. Getting married on a vineyard? Include a case of wine with the wedding date printed on it. If it's a glam wedding, include a loose handful of glitter. If it's a mermaid wedding, rip off a few of your magical scales and include them.

The Wedding Hashtag

Since 99 percent of my brides already work in PR or marketing, I don't always have to explain the immeasurable importance of the wedding hashtag. But since any Tanya, Dixon, or Harri is able to buy this book, I feel I must elaborate: *Branding is everything*. Your wedding hashtag is your brand, your slogan, and your newsfeed all wrapped into one. A lame hashtag gets fewer clicks, therefore fewer "likes" and fewer views—it's like the wedding didn't even happen. Sure, you can use a hashtag that's just *#YourNameAndHisName*, but I know I personally wouldn't click on that hashtag for all the Tory Burch sandals in Southern California (three billion, by my private investigator's last count). And I'm not alone in that thinking.

So here are some tips for creating the cutest, most beguiling wedding hashtag:

✷ UTILIZE YOUR NEW LAST NAME: *#FutureMrsJones*. Since you'll be taking his last name because you're not a lesbian, this hashtag is a cute way to showcase that. A hashtag that combines his last name with your old, soon-to-be-discarded last name is pointless—just as point-less as the temporary surname your father gave you when you were born a female.

✳ USE A PUN OR CLEVER PLAY ON WORDS! Everyone loves puns: *#JonesinForMarriage*, *#KeepingUpWithThe Joneses*, *#NotTheJonestownMassacre*, *#TwoBecomeJones* (in this one you're using *Jones* in a play on the word *one*).

✳ CONSIDER A SPONSORSHIP. If your wedding hashtag is going to drive a lot of traffic, then partnering with a like-minded brand is wise: *#JonesDrinkCoke*, *#BaBaBaBaBaImLovingJones*, *#GotJones?*, *#JustJonesIt*, *#JonesWeddingPlaytexTampons2017*.

Your Wedding Website

Your wedding website is so much more than a place to dump travel and hotel information for your guests. This is a place to let the world know just what kind of couple you and your fiancé are and just how superior your idyllic relationship is to theirs. Again, it's all about branding. What kind of couple do *you* want to be? How you describe yourself to your guests will tell them just how jealous of you they should be. Don't believe me? Why would I fucking lie to you?

In this section I will demonstrate just how much a shift in tone can impact your guests' jealousy levels.

A STANDARD, BORING "ABOUT-THE-COUPLE" SECTION

Mark and Kendra were just two single twentysomethings following their dreams in New York City. Then on January 8, 2014, a chance encounter at a local watering hole brought them together, and they've been a couple ever since. Mark is an industrial engineer, and Kendra is a nursing student. They live together with their dog, Patsy, in Park Slope. But of course you already know all this, since you're invited to their wedding ;)

* Jealousy-inducing level: *low*

A DRAMATIC, PARTIALLY FICTIONAL "ABOUT-THE-COUPLE" SECTION

How does one sum up Mark and Kendra? Mark is an industrial engineer, but he's so much more: a best friend, an omelet maker, a dog walker (even in the rain), a lover of pink shirts. Kendra is a woman, a nurse, a sucker for Anne Hathaway movies, a lover of dark chocolate and good wine. They're so lucky to have found each other. They live in Park Slope with their wonderfully silly dog, Patsy.

* Jealousy-inducing level: *moderate*

AN IDEAL, ASPIRATIONAL, 90 PERCENT FAKE "ABOUT-THE-COUPLE" SECTION

Mark and Kendra are two human beings who found themselves adrift in the bustling metropolis of Manhattan, both seeking Another Soul to call home. It was an average night. They caught eyes across the dark, candlelit tables of some new speakeasy (who can keep track?), and after a few rosemary-infused vodka cocktails and hours of sprawling conversation that touched upon everything from philosophy to spirituality to motherhood and beyond, it was apparent that they had found their Other. They can't help but feel that a Greater Being played a role in their chance encounter. They live and love together with their beast, Patsy, in Park Slope.

* Jealousy-inducing level: *maximum*

See what a difference a little embellishment can make? I know which couple's wedding I'd like to attend!

WEDDING WEBSITE INSIDER TIP

The longer the URL, the better the wedding. Think of your wedding website's URL as your proverbial penis. It's like men with their cars: Women know that the bigger a man's vehicle, the bigger his manhood. Wedding website URLs are no different! So go big or go home! For example, *my* wedding website's URL was www.LauraIsGettingMarriedtoaManandTheyreDoing ItinMayofThisYear.com.

The Not Invited

The unfortunate downside to successfully marketing a wedding is that *everyone* will know about it—and *everyone* will want to come. There will be some friends and coworkers who simply won't make the cut, and this will be completely devastating for them. The simple truth is that the people you can't invite to your wedding will be destroyed, and this is the burden every bride must bear. But exclusivity is what separates your wedding from, say, a stoop sale. This is social Darwinism at its best: Only the strong get invited. (This also is an argument for regular Darwinism—for mating with people you meet at exclusive events to keep the gene pool exceptional. For more on that, see my book *Dating Up: How to Meet Rich Men at Weddings and Convince Them You're on the Pill*.)

But still, we must consider the Not Invited's feelings *just in case* any of them wind up being important someday and you'll want something from them. So here are some helpful tips for letting the Not Invited down gently.

INUNDATE THEM WITH FACTS

FOMOW (Fear of Missing Out on Weddings) is a real and serious condition. When your coworker discovers that she is one of the only people in your department who wasn't invited to fly down to Cabo during the high season for your wedding, it can trigger a powerful case of FOMOW. The best thing to do is tackle it head-on: Approach your coworker, apologize, and explain to her that you have a huge family and so does your fiancé and you're both being forced against your will to invite all your cousins *and* second cousins, plus the venue is tiny because it's a former Mayan temple designed specifically for child sacrifices, and your future mother-in-law is insisting that you invite your fiancé's former nanny, whom he barely even remembers, isn't that nuts? Your coworker will be so over-whelmed with all the immense and interesting details of your wedding that she won't even have time to process any grief.

DOWNPLAY YOUR WEDDING

This one will take some serious acting chops, ladies! It's a nec-essary evil to speak poorly of your own wedding day so that the Not Invited are less aware of just how much they'll be missing out on. So next time you run into your upstairs neighbor who didn't make the cut, before he's even had a chance to say hello, make sure to let him know just how run-of-the-mill your wedding is going to be. Emphasize how mediocre the mass-produced food will be, how the reception will be under a tent so it'll probably be pretty uncomfortable temperature-wise and a total nightmare if it rains, how it's in another state and not near any airports, and that it's being held at 6:00 P.M. on a Friday so you could get the cheaper Friday wedding rates. Of course, you know the truth: that the food will be uniquely delicious, that you'd never dare get married under a tent—

it's more like an elegant open-air house made of canvas—and that your guests will be honored to drive the three hours from the closest airport on a Friday during rush hour because they get to come to your wedding. But your neighbor doesn't need to know that!

FIND OTHER WAYS TO INVOLVE THEM

Just because the Not Invited can't be at the actual wedding doesn't mean they can't still be a part of your special day! Send them links to your registry so that they might participate by buying you a gift. Remind them that the act of giving is the fastest way to boost their mood! Or host a casual engagement party where you can invite a wider range of friends to come celebrate and buy you gifts.

BLOCK THEM ON ALL SOCIAL MEDIA

It may seem drastic, but this is the only way to prevent them from seeing your wedding hashtag. Clicking on the hashtag of a wedding you weren't invited to is a recipe for disaster. It's a slippery downward spiral into depression, a reminder of this and every other rejection you've faced in your lifetime, especially after a glass or two of wine. Blocking the Not Invited is a heroic act of tough love. Plus, that will allow you to post photos guilt-free! Nobody likes a guilt-riddled bride! Doing this will make it easier to . . .

DISTANCE YOURSELF FROM THEM PERSONALLY

This is just a practical thing to do. Forcibly distancing yourself from the Not Invited will not only justify why you aren't inviting them but will also help soften the blow of the inevitable fall-out post-wedding. After all, they weren't there on the Greatest Night of Your Life. What will you have in common with these people anymore? Nothing. It's best to trim the fat early and quickly. Just be sure to do it gently. So, for example, if they pop by your office on their way to lunch to see if you can join them, a curt "No thanks, I'm not eating lunch today" will suffice. They'll eventually get the hint, and while they may be hurt, ultimately the loss of a friendship is way easier to handle than not being invited to your amazing, unique, and special wedding.

FOR THE GROOM

THE MANLY MAN'S GUIDE TO GRILLING A PERFECT RIB-EYE STEAK*

YOU'LL NEED:

2 ½-pound rib-eye steaks (one for you, one for your BALLS!)

Salt

Pepper

A sexy babe! Won't help the steak but it can't hurt to look at her SICK BODY!

2 tablespoons olive oil

1 tablespoon Worcestershire sauce . . . if you're a PUSSY!

1. Remove the steaks from the packaging using your teeth. Leave the discarded Styrofoam container full of meat juice on the counter for weeks.

2. Pat the steaks with olive oil. This will prevent them from sticking to the grill. Use the leftover oil on your hands any way you want! WINK WINK.

3. Generously salt and pepper both sides of the steak.

4. Check out that hot babe's crazy big bazoongas one more time! SICK, BRO!!

5. Turn your grill on to medium-high heat.

6. Grill both sides of the steaks at 7 minutes each so they're still mostly RAW inside, just like YOU! REAL MEN ARE ALWAYS RAW!

7. To be clear, when I say real men are always raw, I mean in an animalistic and manly way, not like fragile or vulnerable or emotionally available in any way.

8. When the steaks are ready, take them off the grill and let them sit for 10 minutes. Then DEVOUR THEM, tearing at the animal flesh with your incisors, pounding your chest, howling at the moon. Let this animal's lifeblood fuel you for another day of working in corporate real estate!!!!

* Original recipe as first appeared in the men's quarterly *Beer, Tits & Cars*

"It takes a village."

—MRS. WILLIAM CLINTON

CHAPTER FOUR

The People Who Work for *You*

With great power comes great responsibility...

is something I just made up. But it rings true because while your wedding day is indeed *your* big day, it is impossible to pull off a feat of this scale single-handedly. After all, does Kim Jong-un maintain such an obedient populace without the help of an entire military? The answer is no. As anyone who has been in a position of great power will tell you, you cannot rule all by yourself. You must delegate, with a clear agenda and a firm hand, to the people who will be crucial to seeing your vision through: your bridal party and your vendors.

While the bridal party and vendors may seem very different (one group is unpaid, like interns or slaves, while the other is paid more than you could ever possibly imagine), they are both here to serve *you* and to help make your wedding dreams a reality. That is their sole purpose, their duty, and their honor.

This chapter will help you manage your legion of assistants as they carry you on their proverbial and/or literal backs in the months leading up to your wedding day.

Teaching Them to Serve: Your Bridesmaids

The tradition of bridesmaids is sacred, and dates back to medieval times. Back then, bridesmaids would dress exactly like the bride, serving as decoys that would distract and confuse any evil spirits into attacking them instead of the bride. So for centuries bridesmaids have understood that it is their job to sacrifice any and everything in the name of serving the bride. Even their lives.

Being a bridesmaid is a blessing and a huge responsibility. It saddens me so much when I see bridesmaids resisting this great gift they've been given by either refusing to pay for their Vera Wang dress, complaining about traveling to Prague for the bachelorette party, or protesting that they can't go to a week-long flower arranging boot camp because they "have to raise their children." Ninety percent of bridesmaids are good friends, and 98 percent of those good friends are sorority sisters, and there's a reason for that: A friendship forged through binge drinking and group sex in fraternity basements means you two have a sisterhood based on blackmail and deep, dark secrets, which makes your sorority sister the ideal bridesmaid.

With this in mind, I always tell my brides not to feel guilty about asking a lot of their bridesmaids. The tradition of lesser women serving a queen or matriarch dates back centuries to the time of ladies-in-waiting. But ladies-in-waiting could never hope to be queen one day, whereas your bridesmaids may some-day be able to ask you to be *their* bridesmaid! (I would say no, though, if they ask—it's a lot of work.) Here are the tasks that are the sole responsibility of the bridesmaids:

1. Planning the bridal shower (more on that later).

2. At the wedding shower, writing down who gave what gift and making a sash or hat out of the ribbons and bows from opened presents for the bride-to-be to wear. This tradition has the humorous effect of making the bride look like a suf-fragette. (As if you would ever consider being a part of that terrorist organization!) Plus, you can hold on to this cluster of garbage to use as a "rehearsal bouquet" at your actual wedding rehearsal.

3. Planning the bachelorette party. This means securing the hotel, transportation, and flights (direct, of course); not-ing the dietary restrictions of all the attendees; if traveling abroad, learning the local language so that the group has one designated translator; researching the best hospitals in the area, should the ayahuasca not sit right with anyone; navi-gating the black market to find the best deals; and arrang-ing for group dinners, bottle service, and of course male entertainment.

4. Securing the penis items for the bachelorette party (penis straws, penis sashes, penis shot glasses on necklaces, penis tiaras, penis piñatas, cock rings).

5. Handling the nitty-gritty tasks that the bride simply doesn't want to do: arranging transportation for guests to and from the wedding; organizing hotel blocks for guests; cleaning up horse manure from the working barn that the wedding reception will be held in; polishing oysters for the raw bar; trapping white doves, which will be released at the ceremony's end; releasing the white doves (this should be done with caution, as they will immediately exact revenge on whoever trapped them in the first place).

6. Making sure the bride is calm and happy on the day of her wedding, which often requires acquiescing to her every whim, no matter how unreasonable, and remaining a friend to her despite the barrage of insults, backhanded compliments, or burns from her cigarette. A bridesmaid is essentially a bride's therapist *and* punching bag, and it all must be endured with a smile.

7. Bedding any single brothers of the bride.

The Wedding Shower

Wedding showers are a time-honored tradition that stems from the days when a father had to provide a dowry in exchange for a younger man taking his daughter off his hands by way of marriage. So a shower would help supplement a woman's dowry so that she might be traded for a richer man who held a better place in society. I think it's wonderful that we still celebrate this beautiful custom even though, sadly, dowries are a thing of the past.

A bride may not need a dowry anymore, but that doesn't mean wedding showers are outdated. Today's bride still needs expensive stuff, and showers are a great way for brides to get all the expensive stuff they so desperately need to fill up their matrimonial homes. The joy of the wedding shower is that it brings all your closest girlfriends and your mother's closest girlfriends together to celebrate the fact that they are buying you stuff! Plus, it's a great excuse to eat some very small sandwiches.

The wedding shower is the responsibility of the bridesmaids and/or the bride's own family, since this is the rule that someone once arbitrarily decided on and thus we must blindly follow. You have every right to expect a shower. And if one isn't thrown for you? Then perhaps gently suggest to your girlfriends that you'd like one via crying or passive-aggressive comments until you get what you want. Here are some fun wedding shower games to play once they realize their mistake!

SHOWER TIME: In the Victorian era gifts were placed into an inverted parasol and then opened over the bride's head, literally showering her with gifts! Since nowadays shower gifts are often kitchen appliances, the partygoers should choose one "Bridal Bummer" and dump all the heaviest gifts on the head of the least popular party guest! This will also let her know that she needs an attitude adjustment before your big day.

BRIDAL BINGO: Create a custom bingo board full of specific details about the bride and groom's relationship—like, where did they have their first kiss? What's the groom's sign? What is his yearly income? What ultimatum did the bride use to finally pressure the groom into proposing? What designer shoes did the groom buy for the bride after she discovered the emotional affair he was having with his massage therapist?

CANDY BAR GAME: Similar to a popular game played at baby showers, this game requires guests to place different unwrapped candy bars inside of men's boxers, causing the bars to melt and become unrecognizable. Then the bride must wash the boxers and remove all signs of the "chocolate skid marks" or she is deemed a Bad Wife. (Or alternatively, if the bride is knocked up and she refuses to admit it even though *everyone* knows, google the baby shower game instructions on your closest iPad and play that instead.)

Your Bachelorette Party

The bachelorette party is another time-honored tradition that marks a woman's final night out on the town as a "single woman" or "harlot," and is another example of something you should expect your bridesmaids to throw for you. Much like a birthday party gets a child worked up, a bachelorette party can have a dramatic effect on a bride-to-be. Expectations are high, which often leads to disappointment and tears. But that doesn't mean you should be holding your bridesmaids to a lower standard; it just means they need to try harder to not disappoint you.

Below is a chart of what is appropriate to cry about at your bachelorette party and what is not.

IT IS APPROPRIATE TO CRY WHEN:

1. People aren't paying enough attention to you.
2. The stripper won't go to bed with you.
3. The stripper is ugly.
4. You realize Atlantic City is a very bad place.
5. ***Your penis crown is too tight.*** ⟶
6. The guys at the club aren't paying enough attention to you.

7. Your girlfriends are fighting with one another and therefore aren't paying enough attention to you.

8. Becky keeps insulting the hotel because it's so fucking obvious that Becky is just jealous because she'll be alone forever.

9. You get drunk enough to finally say aloud the truth that you aren't marrying your husband for love; it's more of a financial arrangement.

10. You just, like, can't even.

11. Any of your girls don't adhere to the strict dress code: You wear white, they wear black—how fucking hard is that to understand?

12. Your SoCo lime shots aren't arriving promptly enough.

13. The rental house isn't as big, clean, modern, fancy, or quaint as you thought it would be.

14. You catch Becky rolling her eyes at the price for bottle service at the club. It's not your fault Becky is broke, so why is she making this all about her?!

15. You find the bachelorette hashtag to be uninspired.

16. You burn yourself with the hair straightener.

17. You don't like how you look in the selfie Becky just posted and she refuses to take it down because she's a fucking bitch.

18. It's mealtime.

19. It's humid.

20. You catch a fleeting glimpse of yourself in a mirror and you don't look as happy as you thought you would be.

IT IS INAPPROPRIATE TO CRY WHEN:

1. A national tragedy occurs during your bachelorette party. It's much more comely to remain stoic during these tough times.

2. You realize how mean you've been to Becky. She did plan the whole weekend after all. But you can't let her know you feel bad, because that is a sign of weakness and she'd just walk all over you like she did in college.

3. ***You wake up next to a strange man and decide the only way to cover this up is murder.***

4. Your selfie stick breaks. They're an embarrassing technology. Be grateful.

Your Vendors

We've touched on wedding vendors a bit when we covered florists. But much like a queen bee ruling over her hive, you can't be served by just one worker bee; you must be served by a whole swarm of vendors. The only difference is that, unlike worker bees, vendors don't come cheap. Wedding vendors typically charge three times more than your average event vendor. And why shouldn't they? They are experts in very specific fields, each of which make up one tiny facet of your wedding. A run-of-the-mill calligrapher cannot be compared to a *wedding* calligrapher— they're entirely different skills. One does calligraphy for bat mitzvah invitations and scroll restoration, while a wedding calligrapher is at the top of their craft, as are all wedding vendors. So it only makes sense to bring together as many of these experts as you can to ensure a flawless wedding. It can be a bit overwhelming to keep track of exactly how many vendors your wedding will require, so here is a handy checklist to help you along the way.

VENDORS YOU WILL NEED TO HIRE

* Photographers (at least four)
* Videographer (you'll need a full union crew)
* Florist
* Caterer
* Baker
* Band (never a DJ)
* Wedding planner (me)
* Wedding design specialist

antique fork rental company

envelopi
(mix of yogi
and envelope
maker)

lace maker

* Wedding dress selector
* Lighting designer
* *Lace maker**
* Calligrapher
* Stationer
* *Envelopi (mix of yogi and envelope maker)**
* Cake topper maker
* Cake bottom maker
* Officiant
* Amish people (to build your barn)
* Elephant tamer
* Babysitters
* Seat fillers
* *Antique fork rental company**
* Masons (to make the jars)
* Celebrity makeup artist and hairstylist

* Backup priest
* Couples' therapist (for the fights)
* Photo booth operator / props stylist
* Best boy grip
* Firework operator
* Organic napkinist
* Artisanal glitter chef
* Live portrait artist
* Juggler
* Mickey Mouse
* Fire-eater
* Fire warden (for the fire-eater)
* Bird enthusiast
* Gazebo architect
* Gazebo destruction expert
* Meteorologist

* Pictured on page 91

FOR THE GROOM

FIND ALL THE GROOM-RELATED WEDDING WORDS BELOW!

```
Y D D O I F O H H F P D W T L
G M D D T D B Y T I N R E T E
J Z C E Y Y L R S D T R X W L
I C Y X M K I D G S G L H L E
B V X U K Z G E O E P Z C R
I O V T Y C A B R O X L H S W
E P U L U Q T T A Y H A D G Y
F N O T F B I F E M M X A N Y
B A E V O F O Y I P X R Z O E
R T C E R N N O A V O W S I M
X I P K D Q N G L A H O W H V
X Y N T R E N I E J A S C G A
C X C G T E G S E J H A O I A
F D P M J K U A I R R O F U X
Q X X C N D S F Y A E E B Y P
```

BOUTONNIERE   CHAMPAGNE   OBLIGATION
ENDLESS   ETERNITY   TUXEDO
REGRET   RING
VOWS   DEBT

> "If anyone objects to this marriage,
> speak now or forever hold your peace."
>
> —UNMARRIED PRIESTS

CHAPTER FIVE

Making Your Ceremony About You

When planning a wedding it's easy to overlook the ceremony.

It's the time when you and your betrothed stand before a minister, county judge, ship captain, or some other human manifestation of the Lord to have your union blessed, thereby making it "official." But it is definitely still the least significant part of the day.

Enjoy walking down the aisle, all eyes on you, because once that's over it's just a bunch of talking until you can get to the party. However, we have learned that traditions are meant to be followed, and ceremonies have long been a part of weddings. Therefore, a ceremony you must have.

Brides can find ways to personalize their wedding ceremonies, just like every other aspect of the day. Make it fun for you! It needn't be a bore, a snore, or a chore you must endure. See what I did there? Ceremonies are so boring that I had to find a way to make writing a w about them fun, so I came up with a jaunty rhyme. And yes, I will now reward myself with a Vicodin-whiskey cocktail for a job well done.

In this chapter I will walk you through your ceremony—what to expect, and how to make sure it's not a dark, dull blip on your otherwise immaculate day.

Going to the Chapel

One needn't have their ceremony in a church, temple, or other house of God these days. Heck, people are getting married on piers, in fields, and even *under trees in parks*! But a majority of ceremonies are still religious, as they should be. After all, why have a ceremony if you don't believe the wrath of God will punish you for not doing it? Here are a few things to consider if you do opt for a religious ceremony.

YOU'RE GOING TO BE UPSTAGED BY GOD

Getting married in a religious space means that whoever is officiating is going to spend most of your wedding ceremony not talking about *you* but about someone else—namely Jesus, God, or Yahweh, depending on what kind of religion you practice. This is well and good on Easter, Christmas, or whatever Jews call Christmas, but on your wedding day this is a bitter pill to swallow and a huge sacrifice that you must make. So prepare yourself.

IT'S GOING TO BE LONG

This is mostly due to all the yammering on about things that aren't you. Again, a massive sacrifice you must bravely make.

THERE WILL BE SINGING

And it won't be a romantic song that serves to remind guests that they're witnessing the greatest love story of all time unfolding in front of them. It will be a hymn, and it may not even be in English. If you find yourself feeling angry, just remember: You will always be remembered for this great sacrifice, and you can lord it over everyone for the rest of your life. (Sound familiar, *Jesus*?)

Acceptable Readings

Many brides choose to allow a family member or cherished friend who wasn't good enough to make it into the bridal party to participate in their ceremony by doing a reading. Allowing them to choose the reading would be unwise. Here are a few classic passages that will make your ceremony more meaningful/longer.

SONNET

How do I love thee? Let me count the ways.

I love thee to the top of our penthouse, to the bottom
   of our glass-bottomed yacht.

I love thee blindly, but only if you maintain your current
   looks. Do not age.

I love thee greatly, in direct proportion to your paycheck.

I love thee freely, and because of the gentle *tick, tick, tick*
   of my biological clock, I love you now, now, now.

I love thee passionately. Unless I am not in the mood.

I love thee very much—otherwise I wouldn't be
   standing up here, would I?

ADAPTED FROM CORINTHIANS

Love is patient, love is kind and is not jealous.

Love does not brag and is not arrogant.

Especially on Twitter and Instagram.

Well, I am not claiming to be humble, or a not-jealous
   person.

I'm just saying that's what *love* is.

But you asked for this

When you got down on one knee.

So when you think about it, if you are ever unhappy

You have no one to blame but yourself.

So rejoice in our truth, and endure with me.

A WEDDING PRAYER

O Lord, please bless this couple, this union.

Please bless them that they might find joy in this new life.

But most important, please don't let it rain today,

For while we rented a tent just in case,

I really had my heart set on taking wedding portraits
outdoors.

Please oh please, O merciful God, don't let it rain.

And don't you dare let the shuttle drivers lose their way.

Should they get lost, may they find their way back to me.

But I will most certainly dock their tip.

And if the DJ plays "Shout" I will lose my fucking shit,
I swear to you,

Because I specifically asked him not to, but he never
emailed me back.

And dear Lord, on this day, when I take that great leap
of faith,

Throwing my own bouquet blindly over my shoulder,

Don't let Becky catch it. Because she always makes
everything about her.

Vows

Vows are a special part of the marriage ceremony, a time when you and your fiancé can participate in the pomp-and-circumstance portion of the ceremony by making generic promises that no one will ever expect you to keep. It makes little sense to waste precious time writing your own vows when you could be devoting that time to selecting a flower crown specialist or something more practical. Here is a template to follow when writing your vows:

I, [*bride*], take you, [*groom*], to be my husband, and I promise before [*god*] and these [*adjective*] guests to be your [*adverb*][*adjective*] wife. I vow to share with you your [*emotion*] and [*socioeconomic status*], and to [*verb*] you in times of [*worst possible thing that could happen*]. As your [*noun*], I will seek to be [*promise you cannot keep*] with you, to forgive you in times of [*type of infidelity*], to encourage you to be [*trait he doesn't have that you wish he did*], and to help you be an [*adjective*] father to our [*unrealistic number*][*realistic adjective*] children. I am so lucky to be with a [*noun*] who is as [*adjective*], [*synonym for* rich], and [*word for "man who I happened to be dating when I was twenty-eight"*] as you. From this day forward I devote my [*body part*] and my [*abstract concept*] to you. *Aaaaamen.*

Dealing with the Flower Girl

Having a flower girl can be an endearing way to incorporate a young niece or secret bastard daughter into your ceremony. But keep in mind that by having a flower girl you are also dressing a young girl up in a beautiful dress, placing a flower crown on her head, and allowing her to walk down your aisle, all eyes on her. In other words, you're creating a miniature bride that you must compete with. Luckily, there are a few ways to help maintain the power balance so that it is always tipping in your favor.

MAKE SURE SHE KNOWS WHAT SHE'S DOING

I can't tell you how many times I've seen it: Out comes the adorable flower girl, and oh, isn't it darling how she barely knows what to do with those rose petals? Look at the delightfully confused look on her perfect, wrinkle-free little face! And later when guests are recounting their fondest memories of the wedding, who do you think they're remembering? That's right: the little flower girl who stole the show by having no fucking idea what she was supposed to be doing. So make sure you have several practice sessions with the flower girl beforehand so that she can make a quick, efficient, and barely memorable trip down the aisle.

NO TIME FOR TEARS

On your wedding day there is only one person who should be throwing tantrums about being forced to walk down the aisle during her naptime, and that's *you*. A fussy flower girl could derail your entire day. Do whatever you can to make sure that not a single tear is shed by her on that day. I find that making very direct threats that you will harm their mommies if they cry works well with young children. So does supplying them with exorbitant levels of sugar just prior to the ceremony, to rev them up and help them get speedily down the aisle. Fun Dip is a great candy to ensure a quick sugar high, especially if ingested nasally.

HER INNOCENCE IS YOUR WORST ENEMY

The child already has an unfair advantage over you, and that's her unbridled innocence and purity. She has not been marred by the evils of this world or marked by the ravages of time as you have. In other words, she is much younger looking than you are. Unfortunately, the spell that the queen used to steal Snow White's youth and essence is in fact fictional, so somehow bottling up her lifeblood is not an option. Instead it would serve you best to never stand beside her and to avoid being photo- graphed together.

On Display

Another important aspect of your wedding ceremony is that you are going to be on display for anywhere from 5 to 180 minutes. All eyes will be on you—not to mention the photographer's and videographer's lenses—which means you will have a lot to focus on. The following tips will help you look your absolute best as you count down the minutes until your grueling ceremony is over.

WALK THE WALK

The moment you walk down the aisle with your father is the first time your groom will see you (unless you've opted to take photos before the ceremony, like a classless heathen). It will be an emotionally overwhelming moment for your groom. For you, this is a time to really focus on walking slowly and to imagine how beautiful this moment is going to look set to Bruno Mars in your wedding highlight reel.

THE PRETTY CRY

Crying during your ceremony is not shameful—it's expected. Give your guests the show they want; make them feel like they're witnessing something truly magical. But don't under any circumstances scrunch your face up, droop the sides of your mouth, or produce any more facial fluid than one or two delicate teardrops. The best way to avoid the ugly cry? Fake it! A quick squirt of menthol in each eye right before walking down the aisle should do the trick.

POSTURE IS KEY

Of course, you'll want to think about your posture while you're standing on the dais or under the chuppah: bust out, butt out, stomach nonexistent. But if your ceremony requires you to kneel, that doesn't mean you can let your posture go. The neck looks most slender if bowed no farther than a forty-five-degree angle. Keep knees together, butt tucked, shoulders back, heart forward, thighs turned inward, triceps tight against your body, biceps firm, ankles taut, and stomach pressed against the back of your spinal cord. And at all times *remain as still as possible.* Hold your breath if need be—this will make for better pictures. And it's all about the pictures.

FACIAL EXPRESSIONS

You'll be expected to react facially to the ceremony, and not just with tears. Some expressions that photograph beautifully:

* LIGHTLY MOVED: Eyes straight ahead, corners of mouth turned up, water in eyes
* HAPPY SURPRISE: Eyebrows arched, slight smile, careful not to flare nostrils
* MISSING DEAD GRANDPARENTS: Heavy sigh, eyes turned toward heaven

Fig 1. POSTURE OF THE BRIDE, KNEELING

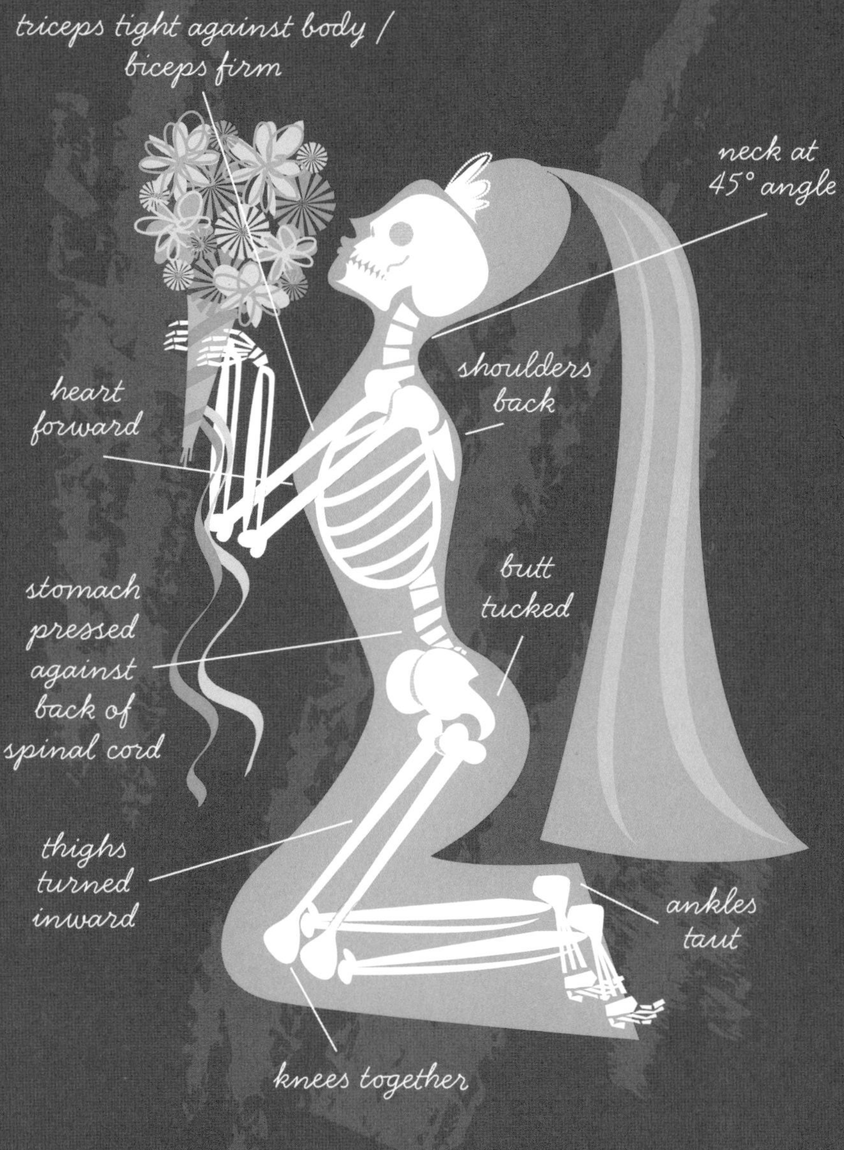

triceps tight against body / biceps firm

neck at 45° angle

heart forward

shoulders back

stomach pressed against back of spinal cord

butt tucked

thighs turned inward

ankles taut

knees together

- ✳ THINKING ABOUT GOD: Eyes rolled all the way back in the head, neck inclined ever so slightly to the *right*
- ✳ BEAUTIFULLY NERVOUS: Ears flattened back against head, tail wagging in short quick bursts, nose alert
- ✳ STOIC ACCEPTANCE THAT YOU'RE THE QUEEN MERMAID AND THAT THE SEA REALM IS NOW YOUR BURDEN AND RESPONSIBILITY: Face expressionless, fins erect, scales shimmering with purpose

lightly moved

happy surprise

missing dead grandparents

thinking about god

FOR THE GROOM

Okay, in this chapter we talked about the ceremony, which admittedly does involve you. Your job during the ceremony is to stand perfectly still and smile unless someone tells you to repeat after them or instructs you to stomp on a glass wrapped in a napkin, or any other nonsensical "religious tradition."

So in order to help you get through the ceremony without fucking it all up, here are some "thinking prompts" for you to ponder while you stand up there. This will keep your brain engaged while your ceremony happens *to* you!

THINKING PROMPTS FOR THE GOOD LITTLE GROOM:

1. *Dinosaurs are the coolest! What are your top-five favorite dinosaurs and why? If you had a pet dinosaur, what would you name him? What do you think the dinosaurs did to deserve extinction?*

2. *Move over, Mario! Video games aren't just about blue-collar Italians falling down pipes and stealing gold coins anymore. Modern-day video games utilize amazing graphics, dynamic characters, and groundbreaking storytelling to redefine how we view gaming as a whole. What's the most important life event you've missed as a result of your crippling video game addiction? Do you have any other life regrets?*

3. *There are so many different kinds of trucks! Trucks do many things: They scoop up dirt and pick up rocks and push around piles of stuff and carry garbage. What are some other cool things that trucks can do? Be specific!*

"Give your body joy, Macarena. Because your body is meant to be given joy and good things. Give your body joy, Macarena. Hey, Macarena!"

—SPANISH FOLK SONG

CHAPTER SIX

Your Over the Top Reception

The reception of your wedding is really the pièce de résistance.

This is the time when you can really go all out—*opulence* is the key word here.

When your guests walk into your reception, they should be blown away. Breathless. Stunned. They should feel small and humbled. They should immediately be overcome with a sudden awareness of their own insignificance on this great green Earth, thanks to the sheer magnificence of your wedding reception. Part of this effect will be achieved by the mind-blowing venue you selected, as well as the six-foot-tall flower arrangements on each table, the giant chandeliers, the smaller chandeliers scattered between the giant chandeliers, the projection of your initials on the white marble dance floor, and the gorgeous window treatments. But greatness cannot be achieved solely by good design and decor. If you're going to throw a party to celebrate the greatest night of your life, then throw a party that will make the Met Gala look like an Alabama Red Cross fund-raising hoedown.

You must think about the guest experience, from what they will eat, to the music, the dancing, the ambience, and the flow of the evening as a whole. Theoretically, you want them to enjoy themselves, but most important, you want them to be *impressed*—even if that means sacrificing some level of joy and happiness. A good party is like a pair of stilettos: They're tiny torture chambers for your feet that can do lasting bone damage, but boy do they look amazing! This chapter will help you plan a night that your guests will never, ever forget—and may even experience aftershocks from for some time to come.

The Band vs. DJ Dilemma

Music is a critical part of any wedding reception. Now I am going to make my first controversial and potentially insensitive comment in this book: Disc jockeys, or DJs, are a tremendous blight on the face of the wedding industry. If I could have them criminalized, I would. If you're going to play music and encourage people to dance at your wedding, do it right: Hire a band. Yes, they are prohibitively expensive. But that should prohibit exactly *no one*. A band is so superior to a DJ that I shudder to even couple them together in the same category. Allow me to elaborate:

1. WOW FACTOR

* **BAND:** I have seen wedding guests moved to actual tears when they walk into a ballroom and are immediately greeted by a ten-person band playing a cover of "Summer Wind."

* **DJ:** A man wearing headphones in front of a laptop? Am I in a café in Los Feliz or at a wedding? I can't tell.

2. GREAT MUSIC

* **BAND:** Everyone knows live music is the best music to dance to. What's more thrilling than hearing popular or classic songs sung by someone who isn't the artist but is at least live *and* alive?
* **DJ:** Sure, they can play all the hits, but so can my Zune. There is nothing impressive about electronic music.

3. LIGHTING

* **BAND:** A band will typically come with their own lighting setup, which can really add to the ambience. Often they will use dazzling colored lights for an extra special touch!
* **DJ:** DJs also provide their own lighting, but they will usually use something offensive, like tacky colored lights. No thank you! This is a wedding, not a Spencer's gift store.

4. MASTER OF CEREMONIES

* **BAND:** The band members will often be the ones to help the evening flow properly between courses and speeches. And they will use their delightful, dulcet tones to emcee your event in style.

* **DJ:** If you've always wanted your wedding emceed by a morning radio talk show host, then a DJ is the way to go. Statistically speaking, their voices are 90 percent more annoying than the average human's.

5. SUITABLE NAMES

* **BAND:** A wedding band will usually have a tasteful name—like The Right Stuff, Rock Doctor MD, Kustom Mayde, or JazzNation—that you won't feel embarrassed to share with friends and family when they want to hire the band for their own events later, after yours is such an earth-shattering success.
* **DJ:** DJs have historically stupid names like DJ Donkieho-tee, DJ Surf 'n' Turf, or DJ Wedding Ballz. Is this who you want to hire as a representative of your taste?

The Table Dilemma

One of the things that many brides get caught up in is the seating situation. Of course, I'm not referring to your guests' seating arrangements—they will sit wherever you tell them and be happy about it. I'm referring to *your* seating arrangement, which is the most important seating arrangement there is. The bride and groom must be centrally located so that all guests can see them and bear witness to their great joy. Nowadays there are many options for how a bride and groom can sit at their own reception, and what you choose can influence your entire event!

HEAD TABLE

This option most resembles a king and queen sitting upon a throne surrounded by their closest advisers, next of kin, and important members of the court. The head table typically sees the bride and groom sitting at the center, facing out toward the rest of the room and flanked on either side by their wedding party. The table should be ornately decorated, although you must be careful that the flower arrangements don't block your guests' view of you (and your groom, if you're so inclined). The head table is often raised above the rest of the tables to create a heightened sense of importance—and so that you may look down upon your guests. If anything, this seating arrangement is the best and truest reflection of the hierarchy of your wedding day.

SWEETHEART TABLE

A popular option, this is an isolated, and often heavily decorated, small table where the bride and groom sit, just the two of them, in the center of the reception area where everyone can see them. It allows you and your husband to sit far away from all the guests that have traveled so far to see you get married. This option also makes it much easier to keep your distance from

the riffraff, and provides you with that exclusive VIP feel and untouchability that you want at your wedding.

BANQUET TABLE

This democratic style of table has become more and more of a trend in recent years, as liberals continue to ruin our great country. Banquet tables are long tables where guests *and* members of the wedding party alike sit together. The bride and groom traditionally sit at the end of the table, which maximizes your visibility but still affords you the opportunity to not speak to any of your guests if you don't want to. Banquet tables are egalitarian, designed to make it feel like everyone is equal, all sitting at one table, but you'll be forced to talk only to the people immediately across from you or to either side of you and no one else. A great option if you have lots of people who are enemies attending your wedding, such as former sorority sisters who have long since dropped the facade of friendship, or your mother and the woman your father left her for, or your father and the woman your mother left him for.

STANDARD ROUND TABLE

Sitting with some of your wedding party and/or family at a standard ten- to twelve-person round table is an option too. This is a great way to come down to your guests' level and make them feel like you're one of them—kind of like when Angelina Jolie wears jeans and a simple tee when visiting Mongolia or wherever she buys her children. While I rarely recommend centerpieces that are below six feet, if you choose this table option be sure that the flowers don't block the photographer's view of you. If the groom is blocked, so be it.

Food

When people attend a wedding there is an expectation that food and drink will be provided, so you mustn't let them down. As soon as the ceremony is complete, your guests shouldn't go more than thirty seconds without being offered food. Immediately following your ceremony, guests will discover that they are ravenously, insatiably starving. This is why the cocktail hour is so crucial: It will determine your guests' happiness for the rest of the evening.

A sample menu follows that demonstrates the breadth of foods that should be made available at your wedding.

COCKTAIL HOUR

Ice sculpture stations

Vodka luge, caviar luge, flavored ice, regular ice.

Sushi station

An assortment of "fresh" sushi and sashimi. This station should be the size of a nice studio apartment.

Raw bar

Lobsters, oysters, clams, crab legs, baby mermaids.

State-of-the-art crudités and seasonal fruits

Celery, grapes, and honeydew nestled in a beautiful, hollowed-out watermelon shaped like whichever state you are getting married in.

Gourmet meat carving station

Premium shanks of the last known bison in the region, panda, endangered mountain goat, or socially conscious slaughtered pig (only the pigs with real bad attitudes get slaughtered; the rest may live).

Imported and domestic cheese and crackers

Imported miniature slates made of whole wheat and liquefied hydrogen and oxygen, baked until hardened; served alongside wheels of what happens when you heat milk, add acid to it, take out the chunks that float to the top, mush that together, and allow to harden and age. Locally sourced, made from organic materials and bacteria.

Italian antipasti station

Gabbagool, mutz, proshoot, sopressat, salam, managoat, stugatz, fangool, mortadell, umbrell, cabatell, stunad, maron a me, amore, a-pizza pie, Moonstruck, olives.

Wood-burning pizza oven

Serving extra large pizzas with severely burned black bottoms.

Personalized pasta station

Heaping servings of noodles tossed in a sauce you've never heard of and served on tiny plates with no forks.

Asian station

A culturally insensitive grouping of foods from various and vastly different Asian cultures, including lo mein, "oriental" stir-fry, pot stickers, pork buns, dumplings, tempura vegetables, and even some samosas in there. Why not?

Food trucks

Pull them right up to the cocktail hour so guests feel trapped in by all the food options around them. Serve tacos, grilled cheese, mac and cheese, lobster rolls, and burgers on sticks, all covered in artisanal sriracha.

Passed hors d'oeuvres

No less than fifteen options of hors d'oeuvres passed around by elusive servers; this allows your guests to utilize their hunting instincts.

OPEN BAR
(available throughout the night)

Should feature a selection of beers, house wines, and premium "women's" liquors such as blue Curaçao, green apple pucker, peach schnapps, Southern Comfort, fermented maraschino cherry juice, and Arbor Mist. For the men, Hendrick's Gin, Cîroc Diddy vodka OR Dan Aykroyd's Crystal Head Vodka (never both), every color of Johnnie Walker, grain alcohol, grappa, three bourbons from small-batch distilleries that have gone out of business, and a nice Scotch to end the night; it must be at least as old as the bride's father.

BUFFET-STYLE DINNER

Unacceptable. Is this a Golden Corral or an elegant wedding? Sure, they're significantly cheaper—which is exactly why they're unacceptable.

PLATED DINNER

After picking and grazing at your cocktail hour, it's possible that your guests may still have a trace of room left in their stomachs. Remember, it is your job as the hostess to ensure that there is no negative space left inside of their intestines.

First course

Typically a salad of romaine with one tomato wedge (not fully ripe) and three carrot shreds.

Intermezzo

Sorbet served in the middle of the meal will remind guests that they're at a wedding, since literally no one else ever does this.

Second course

It *must* be penne alla vodka (not to be confused with the pasta from the pasta station) or some sort of heavy soup, like a bisque or chowder.

Main course

Guests choose chicken (a perfectly dry piece of chicken breast served with organic roasted haricots verts and boiled baby carrots) or fish (a lovely piece of salmon boiled in butter, served with a lemon slice and butter rice with a side of locally sourced sautéed haricots verts) or chateaubriand (French for "whatever part of the cow the butcher had left over," cooked in a red wine sauce and served with green beans).

Dessert

Many couples think that serving wedding cake as dessert will suffice, but this is incorrect. A wedding cake is meant to be admired, not consumed. The venue will cut the cake and distribute slices to the tables, where they will sit untouched for roughly two minutes before being cleared away. In fact, most guests won't even realize they were served wedding cake.

A giant dessert buffet is the only time a buffet station should be present at your wedding, and it should contain cannoli, zeppole, cookies, assorted gummy candies, a sculpture of the couple composed entirely of fun-size candy bars, a "flambé it yourself" station, chocolate fountains *inside* of a fruit-filled hot tub, a front door with functioning doorbell and a server answering the door so guests can "trick-or-treat" if they desire, and a make-your-own-sundae station. An unimaginable array of desserts ensures that no guest will go home hungry!

Speeches

Once your guests waddle from cocktail hour to their tables at the reception, you must give them a moment to digest. This is the purpose of speeches—traditionally given by the father of the bride, the best man, and the maid of honor—they provide your guests with just enough time to get nice and bored. As with every other aspect of your wedding, you cannot cede control and let your speakers have free rein to write whatever they want, because, even though no one is paying attention, they are speaking publicly about *you* at *your wedding* and you wouldn't want them to say anything unflattering. So here is a handy tear-out list of *don'ts* to pass to your speech-givers to gently guide their hand.

Dear esteemed family member/friend/colleague,

You are going to give a speech at my wedding. This is an enormous honor for you, so please treat it as such. You're welcome. Below are some topics to avoid.

DON'T rehash my slutty twenties. I know it's the only remark-able and notable aspect of our friendship history, since we hadn't talked in years until I asked you to be my MOH. But don't. Don't bring up all the nights I spent dancing on bars, don't bring up the Wall Street guys who used to take us out when we were college freshmen in the city, and definitely *do not* mention the marriage I ruined. My mother is sitting right there, my brand-new in-laws are two feet away—my God, do you *hate* me?! Just be cool.

DON'T mention 9/11 unless it's *really* relevant. I shouldn't have to tell you guys this, but . . . trust me, I do.

DON'T rattle off a bunch of inside jokes that only you and I or you and my husband will understand. It's not a speech if only two people understand what you're talking about; it's just a two-person conversation you're shouting into a microphone. If you do it I'll pretend I don't get the joke so you just come across as fucking insane.

DON'T mention either of our past relationships, for several reasons. One, we don't want to highlight the fact that relationships can end, including this marriage. And who wants to think about their exes ever, let alone on their wedding day? No one, you idiot! Plus, I am not over my ex—any of them, really; in fact, I'm looking at their Facebook pages as we speak—so don't bring that up.

DON'T joke about how you didn't really like me at first but then eventually came around. Even if you claim you've come to love me, we know you're a filthy liar and that you despise me so much that you couldn't help but mention it passive-aggressively in your speech and that it's killing you that your friend is marrying a monster. If you're making a speech at our wedding, it's officially too late! Better take another swig of champagne and stuff those emotions deep down, partner!

DON'T highlight the fact that you are sad and alone but that you're really glad your friend has found love. We know you aren't glad. We know you're resentful. And now our bridesmaids/ groomsmen know they aren't going to sleep with you, because you stink of sadness. If you want to be as happy as I am, then you'll heed my advice.

Preparing for Disaster

No matter how meticulously you've planned, no matter how many reminder emails you've sent or how many vague threats you've made, something will inevitably go wrong. The important thing is not to panic, since panic creates unsightly worry lines and wrinkles. Here is some advice on what to do in absolute worst-case scenarios.

THE TABLE RUNNERS ARE THE WRONG COLOR

It happened: You wanted *gold* table runners, and instead you walk into your reception and are visually assaulted with marigold runners. Yes, this is a nightmare, yes, everyone will notice, and yes, your wedding day has slightly depreciated because of it. But the best thing you can do is take your wedding planner aside and quietly tear her a new asshole. Making her feel bad will make you feel better. It won't fix your ruined reception, though.

THE TIMING GETS MESSED UP

Despite the very clear itinerary you gave your band and coordinator, you find yourself being called to the dance floor to do the father-daughter dance *before* the speeches instead of *after*. Now your father is going to be all tired from dancing and it will impact his speech! Remain calm, smile through your dance, shed a few lovely tears, and then quietly let your father know that his speech has been cut. It's better to have no speech at all than a speech that is out of order.

THEY PLAY A SONG YOU DON'T PARTICULARLY CARE FOR

Despite the carefully curated list you provided them, the band has begun to play "We Are Family" even though it was *not* on the list of approved songs. If this happens simply start crying and waving your arms in an exaggerated X motion, signaling for the band to stop mid-song, for guests to stop mid-dance, and for the band to start playing one of the seventy-four Jason Mraz songs you've approved.

PEOPLE AREN'T USING THE PHOTO BOOTH PROPS CORRECTLY

How hard is it to figure out how to use a mustache on a stick? Apparently, it's very difficult, especially for children, and infuriatingly, this can result in sloppy photos. You may find guests wearing the firefighter hats backward or just holding the oversize sunglasses rather than wearing them as they're *clearly intended to do*. Take a deep breath. People are stupid, and there is nothing you can do about it. Simply get another glass of champagne and remember that you can "accidentally" delete all the photo booth pictures if you want to.

SOMEONE DIES

If someone should drop dead at your wedding, it's normal to get very upset, especially if he or she dies before dinner. After all, you've already paid for this person's plate! But this crisis is best left in the hands of medical professionals, who can quickly and discreetly remove the deceased from your wedding so that your guests can get back to celebrating you!

TWO OF YOUR GUESTS HOOK UP

A wedding is a celebration of love, and that can drum up feelings of lust and desperation in people. Mix that with alcohol and it's possible that two of your guests could selfishly use your big day as an excuse to meet and fornicate. Assign members of the bridal party to be on the lookout for any guests who are

getting a little too close on the dance floor and separate them at any cost. After all, only one couple should be making love after this wedding and that's *you* (if you're not too tired, which you probably will be).

SOMEONE GETS DRUNK

While it's mandatory to provide an open bar full of top-shelf liquors, it would be a true abomination if one of your guests dared to get visibly intoxicated. But unfortunately, it does happen. If you discover that someone has imbibed too much of the free alcohol you've paid a lot of money for, you're completely within your rights to totally freak the fuck out. Just go apeshit. Don't hold back. They asked for this.

THE WRONG BRIDESMAID CATCHES THE BOUQUET

Just imagine if Becky caught your bouquet. God, she would be such a nightmare for the rest of the night, flaunting that thing around, waving it in her milquetoast boyfriend's mousy little face, her grating laugh ricocheting off the marble columns of your reception hall, committing auditory assault on anyone unfortunate enough to hear it. It would be just like that bitch to do this on *your night*. No, this cannot happen. Do not allow Becky to catch that bouquet.

FOR THE GROOM

How to make origami out of a wedding cocktail napkin without the help of illustrations because I'm not wasting my illustration budget on this shit:

1. Lay the napkin on a flat surface, like a head table or sweetheart table.

2. Fold it in half so it makes a triangle.

3. Fold it in half again and then you should be able to make a sort of flappy, bubble thing with each corner? It's hard to describe. You can probably skip this step.

4. Okay, it should look like a square now. Does it look like a square? Do whatever you need to do to it to make it look like a square.

5. Fold two sides in so it looks like a diamond.

6. Do some crazy shit that turns it inside out. It should look somewhat vaginal, to be honest. But like a really skinny vagina? Ugh, these instructions are impossible to describe.

7. Um, okay, so at this point there should be two flaps that look a woman's disembodied legs. But you fold those up to make the head and tail of the crane? I feel like I'm missing a crucial step. This is really hard.

8. Maybe just pinch and roll one end so it kinda looks like a skinny little crane head?

9. Just tear the paper a bit to give it wings. I mean, who cares? Origami is stupid. Ever heard of scissors and tape? This is insane.

10. Voilà. A crane made of paper. SUPER useful. But look, you made it through the speeches! Your reception is almost over!

"I'm an enigma wrapped in a riddle . . . and cash."

—REAL HOUSEWIFE ERIKA GIRARDI

CHAPTER SEVEN

Life After Your Wedding

The best night of your life is over.

The last dance has been danced, the favors handed out, the top of the cake put in a box to be frozen, the gallons of leftover food from your cocktail hour dumped in the garbage so no freeloaders can get their grubby hands on it.

Your wedding has ended, and what lies before you is a marriage that you've had little time to think about until now. The good news is that you have a lifetime to think about your choice of partner and whether or not you two get along. However, maintaining a marriage does not require the same attention to detail, finesse, or inflated sense of self-worth as planning a wedding does—and therein lies the problem. For many women, life post-wedding is a sad, dark time. Post-Wedding Stress Disorder (PWSD) is not currently recognized by the DSM-5 as a legitimate psychological disorder, but it affects millions of former brides every post-wedding season.

In this final chapter I will guide you as you transition into the next phase of your life, the years after your wedding, allowing you to live out the rest of your life with dignity as you await the sweet relief of death.

The Honeymoon

Your honeymoon serves as a much-needed respite after the stress and madness of your wedding. But more important, it is your last hurrah, one final Hail Mary to revel in the glory and attention brought on by your wedding. And just like your wedding day, a honeymoon is all about the photos: you and your husband sharing a romantic dinner overlooking the ocean at sunset, your enviable honeymoon suite decorated in roses and swan-shaped towels, you and your husband buying worthless tchotchkes from the "locals," and endless selfies of you and your beloved happily lounging in cabanas as if they were a metaphor for how relaxed and easy your married life is going to be. That's why, when choosing a honeymoon location, it's of the utmost importance to consider its photogenic quality: Romance should be inherent and envy should be induced by every photo you post.

Based on some numbers I made up, honeymoons that take place on a beach are 95 percent more likely to incite jealousy, thus garnering over 300 percent more "likes" than photos of other, less desirable honeymoon locations like Europe, mountains, or quaint New England towns.

The following list offers some suggestions for ideal honeymoon locations that will allow you to really soak up every last drop of wedding glory before the inevitable darkness ahead. And don't forget to soak up that sunshine, too, while you're at it!

* The Ritz-Carlton, Montego Bay
* Carlton-Ritz's Royal Plantation
* The Mandarin Oriental Big Thailandian
* Aristocratic Intercourse Inn & Spa, Turks and Caicos
* Vermillion Derriere High-End Clothing-Optional Resort
* Skull and Bones Club Med Barbados
* Four Seasons Whites Only

* The Secret Underground Disney World Hotel
* The Standard at Sandy Butts
* Depleted Resources Nature Resort, Honolulu
* Sandals French-Cut Thong
* Trump Towers at Suicide Point
* Haliburton Overfished Waters Resort and Spa
* Atlantis (The Lost Mermaid Kingdom)

The Five Stages of Grief

Like a death in the family or finding out that you missed a great sample sale, the end of a wedding can be a time of profound loss. Grieving your wedding is a natural, albeit painful, process. As with regular grief, there are five stages of wedding grief.

DENIAL

For most brides this stage is characterized by a distinct refusal to accept that their wedding day is over and that their time in the limelight has come to a close. Many brides feel numb and emotionless and find themselves posting and reposting photos from their wedding, even when it's not *#tbt*. They'll continue to use their wedding hashtag even though it's no longer culturally relevant and everyone has moved on to the next wedding.

ANGER

Once former brides, now called *wives*, accept that their wedding is in fact over, they turn to anger, which is often general and always misplaced. Anger at friends for getting engaged, anger at their new husbands for being subpar, anger at West Elm for making it so fucking difficult to exchange a pillow cover, anger at the waiter for refusing to serve a fifth Bloody Mary at brunch just because they're sobbing into their vomit, which is on top of their eggs Bene. The anger stage can last anywhere from four weeks to forty years.

BARGAINING

The bargaining stage is marked by regret. It is also known as the "what if" stage because wives are constantly bargaining with the past, replaying their weddings in their minds, pondering the "what ifs." *What if the bridesmaids had worn mint instead of blush? What if the minister hadn't mispronounced our names the entire time? What if I post another wedding photo on Facebook? Will it make my wedding relevant again? What if I just put my wedding dress back on right now and dance alone in my living room, staring at my reflection? Will it be like my wedding day never ended?* Unfortunately, time doesn't work like that. It is linear, and it only moves forward. Yes, even for rich people.

DEPRESSION

After bargaining comes an acute awareness of your present, which is weddingless. You must take stock of your life *now*. You can no longer live in the past, and yet you have nothing to look forward to. This is your life, and it's the life you've chosen. You have no one to blame but yourself. After all, even actual princesses only get one real shot at a royal wedding. After that it's back to the castle to produce heirs and look the other way at the king's indiscretions. As for you, at least you have a birthday once a year to look forward to, although that's not the same. It'll never be the same. Besides, who throws big birthday parties for themselves after the age of twenty-one? Only egomaniacs and Taylor Swift.

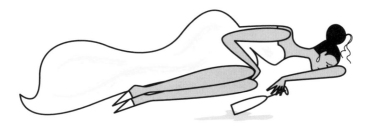

ACCEPTANCE

Depression is perhaps the hardest stage, but it's a necessary stepping stone to acceptance. With time you can come to accept your reality. This acceptance is not to be confused with being okay with the fact that your wedding is over—the pain of a wedding already experienced will always linger. But acceptance will allow you to continue living your life, taking comfort in the small joys: trying new ethnic restaurants, attending Smash Mouth reunion concerts, looking at birds, getting a good deal on Lululemon yoga pants, and watching new shows on Hulu, which you subscribe to because what else are you going to do with your empty days and endless nights?

Or you can avoid all of these stages of depression—or at the very least delay them—by immediately embarking on a new attention-grabbing journey: having a child.

Staying Relevant

After her wedding, a woman gets one more shot to stay at the forefront of her friends' newsfeeds, and that's when she has her first child. (Nobody cares about the second. And your third? They'd be more interested in seeing a photo of what you ate for lunch.) I highly encourage getting pregnant on your honeymoon because a) it'll be the only time during your marriage when you'll really want to have sex, and b) that way you can keep the ball rolling and channel all that leftover relevancy from your wedding directly into baby mania.

Once you can announce your pregnancy, there is so much to look forward to: showers, gifts, baby-bump photos, little shoes, isolating yourself in the suburbs, decorating a nursery, being profiled for your chic maternity style in a mommy blog, and then, if you're smart, monetizing your child via your own mommy blog once he or she is born. For the first year or two of your child's life, you can live vicariously through their cuteness, their adorable lack of survival instincts, their refusal to sleep, and their preference for squatting to defecate. But keep in mind, when their cuteness wears off, so too will your audience's attention span. And at some point you will be forced to face your reality: that you are average. Just another normal person living her unexceptional life. The fairy tale must end, and a new bride and a new mom will rise to take your place. It is the natural progression, the circle of life.

And *that*, my friend, is when you sign up for your first reality television show. And begin the journey to stardom anew.

In Closing ...

You only get to be a bride once (per wedding), so enjoy it, soak it all in, assert yourself, be the narcissist you've always wanted to be. Stand up on the chair you registered for at Pottery Barn and scream "I AM BRIDE!" at the top of your lungs. This is *your* time, *your* wedding, *your* big day. And it will be as special as you are . . .

Unless you choose the cheap table numbers without the sparkles. Then this is basically a barbecue and why am I even here?

FOR THE GROOM

Well, you did it. You defiantly read the whole book. And your wedding is over! Congratulations, groom. Or should I say, *husband*.

My only advice to you going forward is to remain patient, do what she says, give her what she wants, and work hard so you can afford nice things. Knowing your role will guarantee you a successful marriage.

But then again I've been divorced five times, so what do I know?

Resources

A list of helpful books, sites, and favorite vendors, in case this book really isn't enough for you.

BOOKS:

The 7 Habits of Highly Effective Brides, by Stephen R. Covey— This classic self-help book has been adapted to relate to the specific demands and challenges of bridedom. From stress management tips to advice on how to make the tough decisions, like how many different reception dresses you're going to change into, this book has it all.

Eat, Pray, Love, and Exfoliate, by Elizabeth Gilbert—In this highly acclaimed follow-up to her best seller, this is the story of how exfoliating regularly helped one woman achieve smaller pores, fewer ingrown hairs, and a deeper sense of self-worth.

Emily Post's Wedding Etiquette for the Wedding Guest, by Anna and Lizzie Post—An update on Emily Post's original wedding etiquette bible from 1922, this book is geared toward the wedding guest rather than the bride. This guide outlines everything from how to choose what meal you will be in the mood for six months ahead of time to how to navigate a confusing MyRegistry.com site and how to successfully drink and drive, if they prefer not to take the shuttle.

Our Socialism Centered on the Masses Shall Not Perish, by Kim Jong-il—A must-read for any bride struggling with the demands of bridal dictatorship, this book written by North Korea's beloved former dictator infuses hard facts and anecdotal advice with Jong-il's signature wit.

WEBSITES:

TheBrokeWeddingBaby.com—This comprehensive site has resources for the broke bride planning a wedding with a tight $50,0000 to $150,000 budget, including lists of cheap-ass vendors, black-market wedding dresses, and wedding favor factories in China.

AViewFromTheBastion.com—This wedding blog is curated by an actual princess who keeps her identity a secret (although many believe her to be the bastard daughter of Princess Marie-Chantal of Greece and a commoner!). The princess offers her unique insights to any bride planning a wedding in an actual castle, such as how to properly instruct your servants to dust a rampart, how to deal with the ghosts of vengeful kings, and what to do if the moat overflows during the reception.

OnLuLu.com—A must for any bride-to-be, this is a social networking site where women can rate the men they've slept with. Think of it as the Yelp for men. Make sure your husband-to-be isn't listed—or if he is, that his ratings are high.

FAVORITE VENDORS:

Veils, Bales, and Pails—A beautifully curated site that features only the finest organic and locally handcrafted wedding veils, hay bales, and pig slop pails for the rustic bride.

Mid-Wife Crisis—The name is slightly misleading, but this is not a store for medieval birthing specialists. This is a store specially designed for the bride getting married later in life, carrying such crucial items as homeopathic bridal arthritis solutions, Goin' at the Chapel Stool Softeners™, and a motorized Nuptial Rascal Scooter to get you down that aisle faster.

Tulle Time—This is a fantastic wedding dress boutique founded by comedic actor Tim Allen. The shop features tulle dresses handmade by local designers, as well as furniture, decorations, and small structures, all made with tulle. Please note: Tulle-based furniture and structures are not very sturdy.

Dead Rose's Vintage Bouquets—A delightful secondhand store featuring high-end used bouquets.

Neil Blud's Diamonds—A family-owned jeweler that's been around for decades, Neil Blud's has diamonds that are some of the loveliest and cheapest stones I've ever seen. Exactly how he achieves such low prices is a well-kept family secret!

My Wedding Planning Checklist

A comprehensive checklist timeline that covers every step of the planning process to help you juggle all the details necessary to achieve wedding-day perfection.

BEFORE THE ENGAGEMENT:

- [ ] Create a "My dream engagement ring" Pinterest board and send it to him.
- [ ] Create a "My dream wedding dress" Pinterest board and send it to him.
- [ ] Create a "My dream wedding flowers" Pinterest board and send it to him.
- [ ] If he stalls, lay down an ultimatum and be prepared to walk away if he doesn't adhere to your demands.
- [ ] Start picking out your wedding colors.
- [ ] Start researching engagement photographers.
- [ ] Start bribing the Vows contributor at the *New York Times*. It's never too early!
- [ ] Reserve a venue. That'll really put the pressure on as deposits are nonrefundable!
- [ ] Mail out your save-the-dates (see page 65). There is a finite number of Saturdays in any given wedding season, and you want to lay claim to your date as far in advance as you can or you just know fucking Becky's gonna take it.

EIGHTEEN TO NINE MONTHS BEFORE THE WEDDING

☐ Start whittling down your wedding party. If you're having a hard time choosing, holding a *Bachelor*-style competition is a great way to separate the wheat from the chaff!

☐ Hire a wedding planner. Specifically, me.

☐ Ensure that you have the finances to meet your needs. If not, please see page 32 for more on making money appear out of thin air.

☐ Start compiling your modeling look-book for your wedding photographer "go-sees." You want a high-end photographer, which means the photographer will actually be choosing *you*.

☐ Do an intense juice cleanse to shed a lot of weight right away. The sickly and withered-looking body you get as a result will serve as your "base weight" as you begin your bridal exercise regimen.

☐ Register for engagement gifts. Select at least three high-end stores (such as Bloomingdale's, Tiffany & Co., Cartier, or Sharper Image II: The Secret One for Rich People).

☐ Begin the delicate dance that is wooing a wedding florist. Remember, this is like a mating ritual. Demonstrate respect and deference. Never bare your teeth. This process could take months, and one false move will send that florist packing, forcing you to start all over again.

EIGHT TO SEVEN MONTHS BEFORE THE WEDDING

☐ Book the band (see page 112). Or if you're booking a DJ, remember to schedule some time to KILL YOURSELF.

☐ Begin the wedding dress selection process. You should try on NO FEWER than sixty dresses and should appear in NO FEWER THAN two episodes of a TLC reality show about selecting wedding dresses. It is crucial that your dress makes you feel like a princess, as that will help you get into character on the day of the wedding. IMPORTANT: Make sure you're able to ride side-saddle in your dress!

☐ This is also the time to select bridesmaid dresses. Be swift and decisive. Suffer no fools. Spare no expense. Choose an unflattering color.

☐ Block off hotel rooms for wedding guests. To ensure their comfort, order a bridesmaid to spend a night in each of the rooms in the whole hotel. It'll take forever and cost a fortune but it's best to be prepared.

☐ Launch a wedding website (see page 70). If you need help constructing your personal narrative, hire a professional writer.

☐ Begin consultations with your wedding invitation guru. Hypnotism, sensory deprivation chambers, and peyote induced walkabouts are common tools you can use to find your inner invite inspiration. You want a design that truly speaks to *you*. Also, Pinterest.

☐ By now your wedding florist has finally responded to your initial email. That's good. Wait exactly eight days, no more, no less, to respond. Be complimentary without seeming desperate. And don't forget to ask about boutonnieres.

SIX TO FOUR MONTHS BEFORE THE WEDDING

☐ Book the rehearsal dinner venue. The exclusive nature of a rehearsal dinner already makes it feel elite, but remember, the rehearsal dinner should be just as extravagant as the wedding itself! If you're planning to host a day-after brunch, begin arrangements for that now as well. The brunch should be extravagant, too (only the finest of bagels, the most exotic coffee, top-of-the-line orange juice, etc.).

☐ Begin wedding cake design formulation. I always work with an architect when it comes time to design a wedding cake. It should be large and sturdy enough to support a small house. An interior designer can help with the decorative embellishments. Don't worry about tasting the cake, as no one will ever eat it.

☐ Make sure someone is throwing you a shower. It would be absolutely humiliating if no one threw you a shower. If it seems like no one is throwing you a shower, it could mean they are planning a surprise shower. Or it could mean you've made a horrible mistake in who you selected as your bridesmaids/family members.

☐ Check in with your wedding invitation guru. Do you need another vision quest? Has the voice of God told you your wedding invitation truth? Will you go with a seasonal theme or a simple color palette? Museum-quality card stock or iridescent? Don't rush this important process.

☐ Your florist will have responded to your second email with some sort of a test. It may be to obtain a rare stone or commit a petty crime. Do whatever she says. You must succeed at the task at hand or you can kiss your flowers good-bye.

THREE TO TWO MONTHS BEFORE THE WEDDING

☐ Finalize the menu for the reception. When doing a tasting, make sure to sample all the entrees at room temperature, as that's how they'll be served the day of.

☐ Order wedding favors (see page 59). Just to be safe, be sure to order one hundred more than you'll actually need.

☐ Finalize who gives all the toasts, speeches, and readings. It's not unheard of to hold auditions to make sure your father, mother, best friend, etc., are up to snuff.

☐ Purchase wedding rings. And remember, everyone knows that the width of the diamonds in your wedding band is directly proportional to how much he loves you.

☐ Touch base with all your vendors. You should be sending them no fewer than five to twenty anxious emails *a day*. If not, it means you're overlooking something important.

- [ ] Now that your spiritual journey is complete, mail out your invitations. It is customary to give guests two days to RSVP.
- [ ] Now is a great time to enjoy your bachelorette party! (See page 87.) It might be best not to invite that downer Becky, but if you have to, then make sure to slip her some Xanax so she'll be fun for once.
- [ ] You did it. You've managed to prove your worth to your florist. Congratulations! Now sit back and relax as she works her magic. You may request certain flowers, but be warned: The florist will do whatever she damn well chooses. And you *will* thank her for it.

ONE MONTH BEFORE THE WEDDING

- [ ] Follow up with anyone who hasn't RSVP'd and rescind their invitation. You don't have time for their bullshit.
- [ ] Get your marriage license. This piece of paper will legalize and legitimize your wedding in the eyes of the US government. What does that mean for you? Your husband can claim you as a dependent and save a ton on taxes. More money for flowers!
- [ ] Do one final dress fitting. If anything isn't to your liking, crying and throwing a hissy fit is not only permitted, it's expected. It's the only language these dress people understand.
- [ ] Do a veil or tiara fitting. Make sure you don't lose or gain any cranial weight between now and the wedding day!

☐ Assign seating for the reception. A helpful tip for making this arduous task a little bit easier: Don't worry about seating guests with friends or relatives. Just seat them anywhere. Whether or not they have fun at your reception is not your problem.

☐ Follow up with your florist to make sure she has everything she needs to cover every available surface of your wedding in flowers. If she asks for more money, give it to her. If she behaves eccentrically, don't question it. This is all part of the process.

THE WEEK OF THE WEDDING

☐ Send no less than one hundred to five hundred anxious emails to your vendors, bridesmaids, family members, coworkers, former teachers, tax advisors, and casual acquaintances. Just send emails. Make calls. It doesn't matter to whom, as long as you feel like you're doing something.

☐ Delegate wedding-day tasks to the bridesmaids. Who is on veil-guarding duty? Who will bustle your dress? Who will hold your dress up when you have to pee? Who will be willing to take an actual beating if you need to blow off steam? Who will make sure your ex-lovers get text updates about how beautiful and happy you look? It's best to sort this all out so you don't have to worry about a thing on the day of!

- [ ] Have every visible inch of your body analyzed, scrutinized, and improved upon by a beauty professional. Have all unnecessary hairs, dead skin cells, and blemishes removed. You *must* be as beautiful as you can afford to be.
- [ ] Assemble welcome bags for the guests staying in the hotels (see page 57). Have a bridesmaid distribute them, and while she's at it, check each bed for bedbugs. Better safe than sorry!
- [ ] Pack for your honeymoon! Don't forget to pack ten to twenty bikinis, sexy bridal lingerie, and of course contraception! Haha, just kidding, you'll want to get pregnant on your honeymoon (see page 145).
- [ ] Complete the ritual sacrifice of any farm animal of your florist's choosing to ensure the goddesses bless you with ideal weather.
- [ ] Take one final close look at yourself in the mirror. This is the closest to true happiness you're ever going to feel. At this moment your life is full. Enjoy it.

THANK YOU

This book would not have existed without a string of people (mercifully) saying yes to me. Yeses are rare and I am eternally grateful to Erica Finkel for introducing me to my wonderful editor Samantha Weiner, who very patiently guided my hand through this process. Thank you for having a great sense of humor, for being excellent at what you do, and for understanding that meetings are best conducted over a meal. Thanks to everyone else at Abrams for making this book as awesome as it could be, particularly Danielle Young and Jordan Sapiro. A million thanks to Jason O'Malley for being hilarious, immensely talented, and a top-notch Instagrammer.

Thank you to Olivia Gerke, Grace Kallis, and Lev Ginsburg for always having my back and for believing in me. You don't have to but I'm sure as shit glad you do. Thank you Jia Tolentino at Jezebel for publishing the blog posts that inspired this book.

I am very lucky that I have talented friends who are also generous. Thank you to Stacy Davidowitz, Glenn Boozan, and Lauren Lapkus for taking the time to read early drafts; your notes were invaluable. Thank you to Sarah Galley for always being my cheerleader.

Thank you to my parents for your constant support and encouragement; you've been telling me I'm a writer my whole life and I didn't always believe you. Mom, Dad, and Katherine, I owe everything that is good in my life to you guys. Also thank you for your notes on this book. (Sorry I used the F word so often, Mom.) And thank you to the Fanelli/Teague clan for all your love, support, and good food.

And last but never the least, thank you Donny for reading countless drafts, for helping me write all the sports stuff, for putting up with my near constant anxiety, and for being the best friend and partner I could ever imagine. But most of all thank you for asking me to marry you. (Because if you hadn't I wouldn't have been able to write this book.)

Editor: Samantha Weiner
Designer: Danielle Young
Production Manager: Katie Gaffney

Library of Congress Control Number: 2016936637

ISBN: 978-1-4197-2220-2

Printed and bound in the United States
10 9 8 7 6 5 4 3 2 1

Abrams Image books are available at special discounts when purchased
in quantity for premiums and promotions as well as fundraising or
educational use. Special editions can also be created to specification.
For details, contact specialsales@abramsbooks.com or the address below.

ABRAMS
The Art of Books

115 West 18th Street
New York, NY 10011
www.abramsbooks.com